THE BALANCING ACT OF BUSINESS

MASTERING EIGHT FUNCTIONAL AREAS OF BUSINESS SUCCESS

Advantage.

Published by Advantage, Charleston, South Carolina.
Member of Advantage Media Group.

ADVANTAGE is a registered trademark, and the Advantage colophon is a trademark of Advantage Media Group, Inc.

Printed in the United States of America.

10 9 8 7 6 5 4 3 2 1

ISBN: 978-1-64225-249-1
LCCN: 2022903790

Cover design by David Taylor.
Layout design by Analisa Smith.

This publication is designed to provide accurate and authoritative information in regard to the subject matter covered. It is sold with the understanding that the publisher is not engaged in rendering legal, accounting, or other professional services. If legal advice or other expert assistance is required, the services of a competent professional person should be sought.

Advantage Media Group is proud to be a part of the Tree Neutral® program. Tree Neutral offsets the number of trees consumed in the production and printing of this book by taking proactive steps such as planting trees in direct proportion to the number of trees used to print books. To learn more about Tree Neutral, please visit **www.treeneutral.com**.

Advantage Media Group is a publisher of business, self-improvement, and professional development books and online learning. We help entrepreneurs, business leaders, and professionals share their Stories, Passion, and Knowledge to help others Learn & Grow. Do you have a manuscript or book idea that you would like us to consider for publishing? Please visit **advantagefamily.com**.

To my husband whose unconditional love, devotion,
and patience fill my life with joy.

THE
BALANCING
ACT
OF
BUSINESS

CONTENTS

FOREWORD

A great guide for managers …

An easy read loaded with many practical suggestions for implementation.

A manual for use and rereading periodically for reminders and items to consider.

A recommended resource for top managers.

—WILLIAM M. COCKRUM

PROFESSOR, UCLA ANDERSON GRADUATE SCHOOL OF MANAGEMENT

INTRODUCTION

M y first business-improvement insight was at seven years old. After twenty minutes or so of running a very unsuccessful lemonade stand, I began to holler, "Free lemonade, free lemonade!" to everyone passing by. They would walk over with big smiles on their faces, and I would say, "Would you like some free lemonade?" To which the answer was always, "Yes, please!"

I would return their smile with one of my own and say, "That will be five cents for the cup, please."

Most laughed and dug a nickel out of their pockets, a few harrumphed and walked away thirsty, but in the end, my cup business thrived.

At an early age, I had a knack for finding solutions. When I was twelve, I longed for horseback riding lessons, but my parents said we couldn't afford them. That didn't stop me from dreaming, though. I would hike down the canyon to the stables and watch the other kids enjoying their lessons. One daydreamy afternoon, I noticed that the stable workers had a lunch machine with only two options: Cup-a-Soup or old, dried-up sandwiches in rigid plastic containers. Hmm,

I thought, I think I've found my solution. Two weeks later I had my first riding lesson paid for by selling the fresh sandwiches that I made at home and sold to the workers.

When I wasn't trying to figure out how to fund the activities I wanted to do, I had my nose buried in a book. Oh, how I have always loved to read—to learn through reading. My parents would tell their friends that when I was little, it was books rather than soft, cuddly stuffed animals that surrounded me in bed. Books and an insatiable thirst for knowledge have been constant companions in my life. From childhood adventure stories and historical fiction to business acumen and self-improvement, books have always been an integral part of my ongoing education.

Now I have the honor and opportunity to share my knowledge and experiences through my own book. Through the age-old tradition of storytelling, *The Balancing Act of Business* provides information about and understanding of how eight key functional areas of business can work together to create a balance that will enable your company to thrive.

Join me on my journey from Neiman Marcus gift wrap girl at the age of sixteen to the sales and marketing battlegrounds of L'Oréal and Estée Lauder to a people-and-culture awakening at Donna Karan and, finally, to my current role as CEO of Cosmetic Group USA (CGUSA), a company whose revenue has grown by a factor of five under my leadership—growth that was built on the development and success of every member of our team.

I hope my story inspires you to facilitate the success of everyone around you. As a leader, it is your job to engage in conversation, ask active questions, and extract the gems of knowledge that exist in each member of your team so that you can facilitate their success. To do that, you must understand where you stand now, how you can help your team discover ways to improve, and celebrate your team's successes when they occur. This will require increased communication (yes, that means more meetings) because communicating is how we know we are all on the same page and in balance. Strong leaders encourage the sharing of ideas and productive communication.

> **Strong leaders encourage the sharing of ideas and productive communication.**

If you're ready to take a leap into accepting that attitudes and processes may need to change in your organization while also recognizing and celebrating the successes along the way, you'll find the path to doing just that through my shared knowledge and experience coupled with action steps you can take in each of these eight functional areas.

Functional Area One: Marketing

You have a strong marketing team in place. That's great, but it's not enough. A marketing team operating in a silo will not spell success for your business. It's when all departments—sales, marketing, product development, operations, finance, legal, and people and culture—are rowing in the same direction and supporting and communicating with each other that magic happens. Learn how to make the magic happen!

Functional Area Two: Sales

Whether you sell online, in brick-and-mortar stores, or through social sales, the customer experience remains critical and is always evolving. Find out how to stay ahead of the curve!

Functional Area Three: Product Development and R&D

Don't jump the gun—envisioning and developing a new product is exciting, but shiny and new doesn't always spell success. I'll share my techniques for asking the tough questions in collaboration with all your functional areas that will help guide the process.

Functional Area Four: Finance

If your finance department is just a group that receives payments, pays bills, counts inventory, and reports outcome, change it now! The finance team is your best resource for ensuring sales are as profitable as possible—let me show you how.

Functional Area Five: Operations

The bottom line in operations is to discover all the variables that affect profit for your unique business and analyze them, solve for them, correct the process, and gain more profit. Let's dig in to see where your money is going.

Functional Area Six: People and Culture

People want to know that you care about them and are there to help them. This is such a simple thing to do and yet so rarely put into practice. I'll help you unpack how your company is currently facilitating everyone's success and ways to improve that process.

Functional Area Seven: Risk Management

The understanding and relationship you have with your legal representation and your insurance broker are critical. Know how your quality department protects your company, your clients, and the consumer from risk. Don't wait for a crisis to build this important support team—make sure it's in place right now. Let's talk about how to determine if your legal and insurance people are right for you.

Functional Area Eight: Board of Directors

It's lonely at the top! But it doesn't have to be. Your board can help you think through a problem, give advice outside of your board meetings, and be a source of connection to people that can help your company in a myriad of ways. Get ready to see your board as the powerful resource it's meant to be.

Through all the ups and downs of building a business, remember, there must always be celebration, not fear, in the steps you choose to take. Now, let's get started!

CHAPTER 1

TAPPING INTO HIDDEN TALENTS

I slam the stockroom door shut, lean against it, and slowly slide myself to the floor. My immediate goal is to not hyperventilate. I've just told my new cosmetics department of ten team members that I'd be right back, but will I? Yes, I tell myself. I can do this; I just need to breathe and focus. I can hear them all hovering outside the door complaining that there's no merchandise for them to sell, that they can't make any money. They all work on commission, and so they are literally at each other's throats because their livelihoods are at stake. Right now, the way the department stands, none of them are able to make a living, and five minutes ago, they came face to face with the person who is supposed to fix it. Me, who they know as the gift wrap girl. Me, who at twenty is at least fifteen to twenty years younger than every one of them. And me, who doesn't wear a lick of makeup.

So how did I go from a gift wrap girl to being told by the store manager, "You got to get down there and do what you can to help"?

Gumption. At sixteen I had the gumption to tell my store manager at Neiman Marcus that in addition to my gift wrap responsibilities, I would like the chance to manage the store's supply closet, confident that I could do a better job than what was currently being done. That is how my journey to becoming the CEO of a multimillion-dollar cosmetics company began.

Gift Wrap Girl to Inventory Guru

I took a summer job as a gift wrapper at Neiman Marcus, a national luxury department store. At sixteen I was prepared to head off to college that fall with dreams dancing in my head of the prose and poetry of Jane Austen, Daniel Defoe, and William Blake along with a degree in English literature. I also needed to help pay my way through school. My new job entailed chatting with the customers as I wrapped their items with pretty paper and elegant bows, and then I would sit and wait for the next customer to show up. The supply room for all the departments was located in the gift wrap area. This is where the department managers would come to get their register tape and their transfer forms and their pens and pencils—anything and everything they needed to run their departments. More often than not, the supplies they were looking for weren't there. They would go in, knock things around while muttering under their breath, and come out angry and frustrated. I was the first person they locked eyes on, and so they would unleash their litany of complaints on me. I wanted to say, "Hello, I'm sixteen and in charge of gift wrap, and I have no control over your supplies."

But instead I listened and watched for a while and began to visualize how much better the supply closet could be run, so I went to my store manager, and I said, "I want to be in charge of the supplies.

I know I can do a better job than what's being done here, and I need more to do." That was it—I was in charge. Immediately, I flipped how the process was done. Instead of waiting for the department managers to come in search of their supplies, every day I would run around to all the departments, and I would look to see what supplies they were out of or running low on: register tape in the children's department, pens and transfer forms in the men's department. I would make a list, order the supplies that were running low, and deliver the supplies to the departments myself. Magically, gone were the complaining department managers coming to the supply area. This began my discovery of a different skill set than what I was using in my literature studies. When I started ordering the supplies, I set up a spreadsheet in Lotus, and I was able to completely organize the supply chain. So here I was, spending every free moment I had engrossed in Shakespeare and poetry and absolutely loving it but also feeling this innate ability to think operationally and organize processes, which provided me a new challenge and a great deal of satisfaction.

My organizational skills did not go unnoticed, and it wasn't long before one of the department managers asked the store manager why they were leaving me in gift wrap when I could be valuable on the floor, and off I was sent to the children's department to work on merchandising and comparing inventory with sales. Because of the skills I demonstrated with Lotus, they pegged me to track the inventory. I was given huge stacks of the green-and-white striped paper that computer printers at the time cranked out. These printouts showed the store's merchandise. Every item that was received, sold, damaged, transferred, or returned was recorded and printed out, like a checkbook of goods in and out. These I compared to the corporate purchase journals sent in every week from the Dallas headquarters. If there were mistakes made, the comparison of these two reports was where they were going to show up, and the mistakes, if not caught, would throw the inventory off.

I had mounds of printouts that I was supposed to go through line by line, but first I needed to put them in order. So I sat myself in the middle of the stockroom floor and began to organize the printouts into stacks—like the memory game where all the little cards are upside down and you try to find the match. My department manager walked in and saw me sitting in the middle of the floor that was completely covered with paper, and she nearly screamed, "What are you doing?" I told her not to worry, that I had a system and I was going to fix this. I could tell by her squinting eyes and pursed lips that she was beginning to think she had made a mistake in giving me this project. I looked disorganized, and I was taking too much time, and I wasn't getting to all the other things that she wanted me to get done. Now, at seventeen, I hadn't yet had a lot of practice with humility, so I brushed her off, telling her that I knew what I was doing and she needed to just let me do it. And I did do it. I completed the task, and I was able to show how data entry mistakes were being made by data entry personnel at corporate—mistakes that were causing an imbalance in inventory. Because I had done all the analyzing of the merchandise ins and outs and was able to make all the corrections, when we took inventory that year, we had less than 1 percent loss in our department. Department discrepancies can run as high as 5 to 6 percent, so needless to say, the store manager was thrilled.

About a year later, with another successful year-end inventory under my belt, I went back to the store manager, Marion Smith, and let her know that if she just gave me a little office somewhere, I could do this exact same thing for every department. At the time I didn't appreciate it, but now, of course, my adult self appreciates the risk she took on me. It wasn't all roses; I certainly still had a lot to learn.

Marion, a great leader, seemed to know how much leeway to give me and then course corrected me as needed. I was a typical eighteen-year-old, thinking I was doing an amazing job and that I could do anything. But what I didn't know is that I didn't know how to engage with other personnel—I thought it was my place to freely critique each department manager and tell them how to better manage their inventory even though they were twenty or thirty years older than I was and had been doing their jobs for years. You can imagine how well that went over.

I was lucky enough to be inside an organization that believed in the power of people, recognized the unique skills and abilities of their employees, and ensured that they received the training necessary to solve for any gaps they were missing. For me, those were definitely some of the soft skills of how to communicate professionally. Neiman Marcus, through Marion, recognized what I call the next-level leaders, and that is a lesson I still carry with me today when I am building a team and cultivating personnel.

I continued working at Neiman Marcus, managing each department's inventory and, of course, also juggling school, sports, family, friends, and relationships. It was a lot to balance, and there was inevitable crossover between work and school. I'd be in any one of the departments with my stack of paperwork and would then get out my literature book, take a quick read of poetry, make a few notes to prepare for tomorrow's class, and just as quickly, when I heard the distinct click of my coworker's heels heading my way, return to balancing inventory. I always got my work done—both at my job and at school—but it was challenging. Although I may not have been fully cognizant of it at the time, I do believe that period provided me insight that I use today to help employees balance their work with home life.

A lot of companies pile on the work without considering the full person and what other things may be going on in their life or if they are being adequately compensated. When that happens, the employee is unable to produce quality work, they quit, or they become paralyzed from overwhelm. Eventually, something has to give. My experience with juggling school, work, and a personal life provided me a foundation on which I built my philosophy of people and culture in the workforce.

> **A lot of companies pile on the work without considering the full person. Eventually, something has to give.**

Discovering My Destiny

My first year in college, I was just so in love with literature. Yes, I had a job and friends and other interests, but when I looked to the future, when I envisioned my endgame, I saw only literature. I wanted to be in academia. I wanted to be a college professor. I wanted to write. My job at Neiman Marcus merely provided the financial means to get me through school. That first year I took a wide array of core courses, like economics, philosophy, algebra, political science, and, of course, English literature, which helped me further confirm the new skill set that I had first stumbled upon as a gift wrap girl turned supply-closet organizer. As it turns out, I excelled in economics and logic.

My second year was when I declared my English literature major and chose to minor in business administration. That's when I began learning about business law, marketing, and human resources on a general level as I worked my way through each department's merchandising checkbook, so to speak. By the end of the second year of my inventory reconciliation work, the entire store had gone from a

4.5 percent loss to a 1.5 percent loss. Corporate began to question how this was possible. Fortunately, I had all my records of what I had been doing, and they had records of me constantly calling and making them aware of the errors that needed to be adjusted. Once they realized that we weren't cooking the books somehow, they asked me to write the procedure for the rest of the company. I was shocked and honored at the same time. It was great to be recognized and to put my writing skills and what I would later realize were my teaching skills to use.

My success with inventory reconciliation granted me a spot in the Neiman Marcus executive training program. The program was all about how to lead and to think differently. It provided me a window into who I was as a leader. Now, at twenty, with a few executive training sessions under my belt, I was talking with my store manager, Marion, about our cosmetics department manager, who had tragically passed away from cancer. I had not engaged with that department, since that inventory was not purchased centrally from Dallas. The department manager calculated need, received corporate approval for purchase levels, and negotiated directly with each cosmetic and fragrance brand representative, finally writing the orders that kept the department properly stocked. Marion had tried to keep up, but with her busy schedule, appointments were canceled, unapproved orders stacked up, inventory dwindled, and tensions were high with the commission-based salespeople. Unbeknownst to me, Marion was preparing me for her next words: "I know you can fix this; I need you down there now." There was no training, no orientation, no introduction to my new department or responsibilities. I simply headed to cosmetics, eager to solve the problem.

As I purposefully approached the department, I felt the tension, saw the poor state of half-empty counters and shelves, and, when all eyes turned toward me, I lost my confidence. They were not welcoming eyes ushering me into the fold. They were eyes of frustrated salespeople who were at each other's throats and those throats of anyone else they held responsible for the department's demise. These team members knew me. I had been the gift wrap girl. They knew me from store functions and employee parties. They knew I was going to school. What I saw on their angry, confused, and hungry faces was one question: "What are you doing here?"

Okay, deep breath. "Marion sent me down to turn around the inventory here and get sales moving again." Pure silence. Then, like out of a nightmare, hysterical, incredulous, now-the-world-has-certainly-come-to-an-end laughter. As though I didn't exist, they all started to criticize Marion's management and judge my youth and untried skills. The gift wrap girl? More hysterical laughter.

My mouth felt suddenly dry. "Marion sent me down to help you all out."

"She's going to help us? That's a laugh," said one woman while pointing at me.

"We don't need help gift wrapping—we need product to sell!" another one chimed in. "Do you have any product for us to sell, Andrea?"

I felt like I was back in elementary school, not good enough to be picked for the dodgeball team. I did not belong on Team Cosmetics.

"Yeah, that's what I thought," she replied.

Then they all turned their backs to me, tittering away, trying to decide what they were going to do.

Embarrassed, feeling inadequate, and wanting to hide it, I said, "I'm just going to check on something in—in—in the stockroom. I'll be right back." It took everything I had not to sprint across the floor. As soon as I reached the stockroom door, I yanked it open and stepped inside. I took a quick look back and found the whole group marching my way. I slammed the door shut. And that's how I found myself hyperventilating on the stockroom floor of the cosmetics department.

Eventually, I mustered up the courage to ease the stockroom door open and confront the frantic people who now depended on me to make a living. They needed to sell merchandise, and I needed to figure out how to provide them that opportunity. In that moment in 1984, they wanted La Prairie, Lancôme, and Chanel on the shelves because that's what was selling, but we didn't have enough of those brands, and I didn't have the power to get them there quickly. I told them all that I would figure it out but that I needed time to do so, and in order to provide me that window of time, they needed to sell what was currently on the shelves. No matter how long the product had been sitting, it was time to dust it off and get creative.

I walked them over to the fragrance counter, pulled down a bottle of perfume from the top shelf, and said, "You see this bottle of Joy by Jean Patou? It costs $300, and a 10 percent commission on $300 is a good amount of money, so let's focus on selling items like this." I immediately reached out to the rep for Jean Patou and to other fragrance company reps to pull some promotional moneys from them to run a targeted marketing program, and then, drawing on what I learned in my marketing courses at college, it was time to determine how we would get people to buy luxury perfume as quickly as they had been buying blush, lipstick, and foundation. I worked with the other departments, leaning on the relationships I had built there during my inventory days. I would go to the suit department and tell them that for every customer they sent to us who bought a fragrance we were promoting, I would give them five dollars. That five dollars came from the fragrance rep, so it didn't cost my department a cent.

I went through our existing inventory this way, putting together individualized promotions and marketing plans. To my surprise, the buying side was much like running the supply closet, simple supply and demand economics, and I began to use my newfound knowledge of logic to push back on headquarters' rationale for lower approvals on orders than was necessary for us to gain sales traction. I spent many appointments with brand representatives convincing them to spend their promotional budget on our little department rather than on the big stores in Orange County and Los Angeles. I was also learning about sales projections, inventory turn, "open to buy" based on budget, which was based on sales (which were hard to come by with the status of our inventory). This was also where I honed my sales skills, learning how to discover the motivation to buy and close the sale.

Drawing on the marketing skills I learned in my business classes and the leadership skills I learned through the Neiman Marcus training program, the cosmetics team and I turned the department around over the next four years. I showed them that they could trust me, and that was the key. That trust empowered them to open themselves up to new ways of selling and to adapt to new automated processes for tracking and transactions. The success of our work received a lot of attention and resulted in a significant expansion of our department's floor space.

Shakespeare or Sales—Time to Choose

By the time Neiman Marcus's cosmetics department was flourishing, I had completed my undergraduate and master's degrees, and I was teaching college-level literature. It was part time. At twenty-two and fresh out of school, I wasn't being offered tenure, but it was the start of the life in academia that I had always dreamed of. I taught English literature and drama—not the actual acting, but the reading and meaning of drama, of Shakespeare—two days a week. I was enamored of teaching, but I was also eager to make money in order to pay back my loans, which was something I couldn't do on a part-time professor's salary alone, and so I continued working in the cosmetics department at Neiman Marcus full-time.

The success of the cosmetics department continued and began to grab the attention of some of the brands that we were selling well. We weren't Beverly Hills Neiman Marcus. We were a little store in a resort area of San Diego, and suddenly these brands were seeing a significant increase in the volume and revenue of their lines in our little store. The executives of Cosmair, a division of L'Oréal (now L'Oréal USA), Estée Lauder, and others started to come by the store to see what was happening and how it was happening. They were wowed by our new, large island of cosmetics in the middle of the store, which continued to expand.

At that time L'Oréal was creating a brand-new division, and they were looking to populate that division with people they felt could do the job. One of their reps who had been through the good, the bad, and the ugly with me recommended me for a job. Now, as I was interviewing for and considering this new opportunity with L'Oréal, Neiman Marcus was asking me to move to Dallas to finish my executive training program with them. This was where the rubber met the road. I had some significant decisions to make. Should I stick with academia and continue chasing tenure and teaching Shakespeare, go to work for L'Oréal, or stay on my solid trajectory with Neiman Marcus?

This was another moment in which I am grateful to Neiman Marcus for the patience and flexibility they showed me. I asked them to let me go to Dallas to visit for a little bit and get a feel for the area and the community. It turned out Dallas in the '80s wasn't a good fit for me. I'm a San Diego girl. I grew up in a laid-back culture of surfers, and Dallas felt like the polar opposite. The L'Oréal job, on the other hand, would require a move to Los Angeles, which wasn't San Diego but still had a casual California vibe. A final piece of the puzzle was that the surfer and drummer whom I intended to (and did) marry had just been accepted into the Musicians Institute in Los Angeles.

Even though I was working at Neiman Marcus, teaching, and working a third job at night as an inventory counter, I was still struggling financially. I will tell you honestly that I went for the job that paid me the most money because I was trying to pay back all my college loans as quickly as I could. L'Oréal paid three times what Neiman Marcus was offering me. My thought was, I can do the L'Oréal job for a little while, pay down my loans, and then return to academia. Teaching in academia was still my endgame. Telling my freshmen students that I was leaving was so hard. They wanted to be able to take level two of what I would be teaching next. I kept telling them, "Don't worry, I'm coming back. I'll be gone for a couple years max." And I truly believed I would.

In the End

I never did return to academia. I enjoyed a successful career with Cosmair/L'Oréal, and then I was recruited by Donna Karan. My experience at the Donna Karan Beauty Company was what brought together all the functional areas that I am going to share with you in the following chapters. The reason this experience was so pivotal for me was because I was part of a leadership team of six women brought in to help launch her beauty company from the ground up. We all came from corporate, which was like being in the army. With Donna Karan, you felt like you were in Bohemia. All the external structures of a big corporation were gone. We were no longer cogs in a wheel who performed as was dictated from the top down. Donna's perspective was, "You guys are the experts, figure it out." We were responsible for the big picture and for getting into the weeds to make the big picture happen—a once-in-a-lifetime opportunity that cultivated my progressive turnaround CEO philosophy of balance and harmony.

Eventually, I took all the knowledge, skills, and experiences I collected from Neiman Marcus, L'Oréal, and Donna Karan and founded my own CEO consulting firm, which allowed me to combine my business abilities in these eight functional areas with my love of teaching. Today I'm thrilled to be able to expand my opportunities to teach through the lessons I offer in my book.

Now, let's get started with marketing.

CHAPTER 2

FUNCTIONAL AREA 1: MARKETING

I park my car, turn off the ignition, and say, "Go get 'em" to my reflection in the rearview mirror. It's my first day with my new consulting client, and I'm excited. I stride across the parking lot with a spring in my step on this sunny California day. As I pass the loading docks, I am met with stack upon stack of product-filled pallets that seem destined for nowhere, with their once tightly wrapped plastic now drooping in despair. The docks are eerily absent of life, and I hear angry rumblings coming from my right and turn to look. What I had thought was a lunch truck when I pulled in is, in reality, a check-cashing truck that for a 1 percent fee will cash payroll checks for employees worried that the company might bounce the check. This is not good. This is not good at all. I knew when I took this client on that there would be challenges. It's 2010, and many companies are still recovering from the recession—but this does not look like a company that's recovering. This looks like one that's closing. I take a deep breath and walk through the front door determined to find out what has gone wrong and how to fix it.

Two People and a Bag of Tricks

The owners of the company, one a salesperson turned operations leader, Al, and the other a hair stylist turned product developer, Judy, built a thriving $18 million company by working closely with their contacts from previous careers, great ideas, and the ever-present product innovation.

The business plan consisted of Judy imagining, "Why hasn't anyone ever …" (fill in the blank) and Al figuring out how this never-done-before product could be industrialized. Al and Judy would hit the road with their bag of amazing tricks, color-changing lipstick, three-dimensional hot-pour designs, lip products that stayed put for hours and never transferred to cups or glasses when the one wearing them took a drink: amazing! They would convince customers to buy by tapping into their industry relationships, taking risks, relying on charisma, and of course using their scrappy sheer force of will. Once the 2008 recession hit, they didn't adjust their process to the new market, and their business started to severely decline.

My first meeting with the leadership team was eye-opening. They recounted the horrors the company had faced due to the recession's impact. All the cuts that had been made, the ragged state of raw material inventory, hundreds of thousands of dollars in orders that would never ship to now-bankrupt clients, loss of talent either through layoff or resignation due to having found more fertile ground, the thin book of business left, and the rock-bottom team morale. But that wasn't the worst of it. Those were merely the consequences of the worst of it. It soon became clear to me that the company was not able to rebuild because its previous success was built on a small, finite funnel of relationships. Those relationships were with people who were now gone, having pulled their manufacturing in-house or been laid off or relocated to other companies as a result of the recession.

I cautiously asked about their previous and current marketing efforts. My inquiries were met with incredulity. "Marketing?! We tried it once, and it was a waste, and we certainly can't afford to do it now."

Marketing is the fertilizer that makes sales grow. Without it, sales will wither and die over time. My client had no marketing in place.

This was the reason the company was not rising two years after the recession. The

> **Marketing is the fertilizer that makes sales grow. Without it, sales will wither and die over time.**

people who replaced their customer contacts didn't know the company; through postrecession mergers and acquisitions, their contacts were no longer in the same positions of power; or, more deadly to a company, their contacts did not want to risk their *new* job working with a company suspected to still be struggling to recover. It really was that simple. The new contacts didn't know the why, the who, the what, or the where, or if they did, the messaging they heard was one of dire straits. Each time there is turnover in a client company, your marketing message is there to fill the gap and provide the newcomer context: Why should she keep buying from your company when she has contacts at another she knows and trusts? What else do you make? Who are her contacts there? Where do you sell? Without marketing, a company can only hold on to a client for so long when client staff turnover happens—imagine such turnover happening to the majority of your clients *all at once*!

The battle for marketing was hard won. Here was a company trying to rise out of a spiral toward bankruptcy with custom-produced products sitting on the dock unable to be sold because the clients they were made for were now out of business. There was barely enough cash flow to buy raw materials for a thin string of actual orders, and the struggle to make payroll each week was real. The two founders each had a skill set—one was operations and the other product development—and both were fighting for the survival of their company with those two skills alone. And here I was, asking them to spend precious pennies on the expensive, nebulous creation of ideas called marketing? What?! I saw the whites of Al's eyes that day, made more prominent by the red of his angry face. Not one to back down, even when my consulting value is in question, I set off with a few paper clips, a ream of paper, and a roll of duct tape (my survival tool of choice). I was out to show the power of marketing.

Sparketing—Yes! It's All Connected

"Sparketing!" Gimme an S! Sales! Gimme a P! Product development! Mix it with marketing! Sales—product development—marketing! Go, fight, win!!! You guessed it: marketing is a team sport. When these three departments are in balance, I call it *Sparketing*. Why? Because it feels like magic is happening. Hero product after hero product is launched, sales soar, awards are won, congratulations are given, market share is gained, companies grow. Wouldn't you like a little magic?

One of the founders of my new client company could sell anything, so what did they need marketing for? "I don't care if the customer wants/needs it! We can sell it in!" "I don't care if we have not industrialized it! Once I sell it, we'll figure it out!" *Man Sells Forty-Foot Yacht to a Saharan Nomad.* The other founder's strength was product development. Her form of marketing was about the product. Make an item that fills a gap in the marketplace out of top-tier materials and describe it well enough, and of course the clients will want to buy it. If not, well, send in Al to close the deal with favorable pricing … they didn't need marketing. Sound familiar? If it does, beware: your clients are on the verge of sales fatigue, your finance team is about to get extremely nervous, and your company is already losing market share. Product development can't do it alone, and when the sales pipeline starts to shrink, there is nowhere to sell these amazing products. Marketing is a team sport. Marketing asks the questions, analyzes the input, and generates the magic that turns a soot-covered Cinderella into a princess who marries the prince and lives happily ever after. Imagine her life without that magic!

This company was out of fairy dust, and it was time to get down to business and start asking the tough questions, align the founders to the cause, and get busy making magic.

Where to start, though? At the very beginning, of course. "Who are you as a company?" That's the question I asked each of their sixty employees across seven departments. I received sixty "Huh?" responses. I then followed up with more specific questions. What does the company do? What is it known for? Who are the customers? What does the company make? Why do you think the customers buy from the company? Would you buy from the company? The spectrum of answers to this type of company-wide survey can either open a Pandora's box of issues or confirm that your employees are all rowing in the same boat.

Once my extensive questioning was complete, I recorded each employee's answers on a dedicated page to later record leadership's responses to them, paper-clipped them by department, and then bound them all together with duct tape. Yep, duct tape. I admit it was a bit dramatic, but I needed to prove a point to the founder, who believed marketing was a waste of money. I just created the beginnings of a marketing manual with paper clips and duct tape—nothing fancy, flashy, or expensive here—a marketing manual that became the backbone for the internal and strategic messaging that eventually turned into ads, collateral, and industry events.

Here's a sampling of some of the responses that shows the diversity of perspectives depending on the employee's role in the company.

Assembly line: "I don't know. We are always in a rush, starting and stopping, changing the schedule, adding a second shift, then abruptly going back to one. It feels like chaos around here. We just keep our heads down, nose to the grindstone, and pray we make the looming ship date."

Quality assurance: "We are incredibly strict. I came from pharmaceuticals, and cosmetics only go on your face, so our testing standards are super tough."

Finance: "Well, soon it won't matter what my answers are. We are on the path to bankruptcy because we sell everything so cheap."

R&D / product development: "We use top-tier ingredients from the finest suppliers around the world, making our products top notch."

Sales / customer service: "Our customers love us! We are the fun company."

At my next leadership meeting, I read the responses aloud, with an edit here and there, as though I were a customer talking about that company. The goal was to see what the founders believed was true, didn't know, or never thought about, and to define the company promise. My presentation was met with a lot of heated discussion and arm wrestling with Al. He argued that they were a business-to-business (B2B) organization, so they didn't *need* marketing, that marketing was just a spin on what sales and product development actually accomplish, and, of course, that marketing was a waste of money.

Armed with a clear understanding of how the founders viewed the company *and* how their employees viewed the company, I was ready for the next step: finding out their customers' view of the company, its product, and its services. Much more daunting to ask one's customers these questions? Yes. Worth the fear, uncertainty, and truth? You bet. Once you know the perspective of all the players—owners, employees, and customers—you can develop a message that is true and that resonates with your target audience. Now you're ready to create your first basic marketing message, revamp the one you have, or realign the team around who the company needs to be to succeed. We asked the client what we were doing well for them and what we weren't. Would they recommend us as a company? Did they think of us first?

In the end we did define the company's promise:

The company promises an excellent experience, outstanding custom products, and unparalleled value, delivered on time.

Sometimes You Gotta Guerrilla

The old adage that you can lead a horse to water, but you can't make him drink applied here. As a consultant for The Color Factory, I had to provide value where the client wanted it—which unfortunately, in this case, was not marketing. Fight as I might, it was a couple of years, a change in ownership, and changing the name to Cosmetic Group USA that allowed the go-ahead for any kind of traditional marketing. So I refocused on operations, supply chain, and cash. All the while, however, I was a guerrilla marketer, marketing to the employees, creating more guerrilla marketers as I went, and slowly getting the message out to clients through direct personal marketing. The employees were already part of the budget, so no extra expense was incurred. More on this later.

Analytics and Budgets

You have your message; now how do you get it out to the people who need to hear it? Ads in industry publications, in-person events, website and search engine optimization, social media and engagement, guerrilla marketing tactics, printed collateral material, all of the above? How do you choose? Do it all in-house, hire a marketing firm? The answer is found in analytics and budget.

ANALYTICS:

Analytics is the systematic computational analysis of data or statistics. It is used in order to discover and interpret meaningful patterns. Companies use the results to make better-educated, more effective decisions. How do you know what to analyze? Most companies sell either a product or a service. These are sold to another company (business to business) or to the end user (direct sales). The bottom line is that they are sold to people. People with bosses to please, budgets to work with, risks to avoid, and satisfaction to be had. Thanks to social media, we can know quite a bit about people and companies long before word one is spoken between us. This is front-end analytics, looking at data that helps you decide what you will do. Back-end analytics is how well you performed once you implemented your plan.

On the front end, ask yourself this:

Who are your customers?
>> **Are they digitally adept or old school?** Do they exist only in your industry, or is there potential outside of your industry? (Does your company sell garden tools? Think a celebrity known for rock and roll music who launches garden tools. Or are you Black & Decker? Think launching the latest scent for men.)

Where are your target customers?

» **Trade show:** Which ones, how often do they go, whom do they send? Some of the best advice I received was to go to a trade show or conference that has nothing to do with your industry. The benefit? Potential customers your competition may not be thinking about. Identify common denominators among your clients and potential clients. If interest in a new type of trade show pops up, research it, attend as a guest, determine the value, and invest in exhibiting or not, based on your analytics. If the who's who of your client base is shifting in that direction, make sure you are there to greet them.

» **Online:** What sites do they frequent, and what things do they like or show interest in? For each client company (we are talking B2B cosmetics here), there are counterparts for every department and leadership level. Connect with these individuals on LinkedIn, Instagram, wherever they are on social media. If, based on their posts, one of your client's staff in product development loves everything black, maybe you send your next marketing collateral wrapped in amazing black paper. If the client's mascara and eyeliner branding is all about *black is the new black*, maybe you can echo it in your company's sample collateral messaging to them. Personalize your marketing efforts as much as you can. Find out what your potential customer is doing online. Already a customer? There is nothing better than direct in-person marketing, but make sure you know your message. It's always about what they heard and understood, not about exactly what you said. Their word of mouth is priceless, so you want to make sure they heard it right.

Back-end analytics: How are you performing as a company?

» At CGUSA, I set up dashboards that showed what percentage of shipments were delivered on time, how many times a custom product was approved on the first sample delivered to the client, how many redirects there were, and how many customer complaints about the product were received. Then we moved our analytics to the outside world. What were end users saying about the products we made for our clients? Were they winning industry awards, were the bloggers and YouTube independent reviews positive, were our clients' launches successful, how many of our products were the top selling in their category in retail stores? How many were "trending" online? And finally, we moved into industry trends. Forecasted trends (I seek out packaging designers who are often two years ahead of the products that will fill them) and helpful analytics of public companies can be found in their corporate filings—this is where you'll find targeted clients and your competitors. These public organizations were more than one hundred times CGUSA's size and had most of the work done by an outside agency, but it was still valuable information in developing our marketing strategy.

Keep your eye on potential industry shifts as well. At CGUSA we watched as Johnson & Johnson battled the talc lawsuit. Cosmetics contain talc, which is difficult to replace in powder cosmetics, like eyeshadow and blush, because of its velvety texture, low cost, and role as primary ingredient. Since CGUSA is a California-based company, we operate under state regulations that limited the way in which talc was used in formulas or required the packaging to warn customers that exposure to this product could cause cancer. Imagine, cigarettes *and* cosmetics may kill you?! No client of ours wanted that warning on their product, so we started developing without talc. As the Johnson & Johnson lawsuit escalated, there was a rush for talc-free products, which we were positioned to fill. Issues faced by the giant corporations can sometimes help smaller competitors gain market share.

Now you know who your clients are, what they are doing, and how you as a company measure up, but how do you market to them? Remember that marketing is a team sport. You've asked questions and done the analytics; now onboard your team: sales, product development, finance, operations, quality. The data from within your own company will ensure your messaging hits its mark. Does your quality leader have development information that was discussed in a quality meeting that might help marketing better target the message? How about the operations leader? Finance? You will be surprised how relationships from every departmental head will help your marketing team target the right message.

The biggest challenge with low-budget (or no-budget) guerrilla marketing is getting your team to do the work. After all, they didn't join the company to be researchers and analysts. Most department leaders think they know what marketing is, and they know that (1) it's not their job, and (2) How would they know how to help? It's a bit daunting to be asked to help marketing do its job, and you're in finance: What? One by one, though, as they begin to see that their counterparts are coming forward with data and anecdotal stories that seem to support marketing's need, the rest of the team will join in. Then you are firing on all cylinders and have a path forward to build your multilayered marketing effort.

BUDGETS OR THE LACK THEREOF:

There are many variables that dictate a marketing solution or plan. Budget is certainly at the top of the list. Little or no budget doesn't mean marketing can't exist. You just need to be more creative with what you already have. It may be that you do not have a dedicated staff member responsible for marketing. If not, assign someone even if they are not the perfect person or have other responsibilities. Create a brainstorming group that includes several team members. These team members use marketing skills every day; we just don't call them marketers. Let's say operations and quality have been locking horns. Sales and operations are in a meeting, and operations gives sales an example of how "QC gets in the way." Sales had recently met with a client that raved about the company's attention to detail and quality, and shares this with operations. What just happened? Sales *marketed* the features and benefits of their own quality control team directly to an internal team member! Once again, it's all connected! The next time the ops person is on a call with his counterpart at that company and he's getting flack for timing or pricing, he has marketing points about his company's top notch quality to share with that counterpart to redirect the tense conversation.

> **Little or no budget doesn't mean marketing can't exist. You just need to be more creative with what you already have.**

Identify current marketing messages that all your team members may not be aware of, and share them! Your team is your best amplification tool. Direct, in-person marketing is what happens when people gather at industry events with potential clients, existing clients, support vendors, and competitors. Make sure everyone is clear on what that messaging is, specific to the audience you are targeting. Do you want to get the word out that you're doubling your capacity soon with a new building, that you are patenting a new product and are looking to launch with a partner retailer, that you have increased your product development team by 50 percent to support new projects? Pinpoint your strategic message and then strategically share it. You tell two friends, they tell two friends, and so on. Your team will plant the seeds, and word-of-mouth marketing is the fertilizer that will make the sales grow.

Marketing Is a Team Sport!

You have a strong marketing team in place. That's great, but it's not enough. A marketing team operating in a silo will not spell success for your business. It's when all departments—sales, marketing, product development, operations, finance, legal—are harmonizing and supporting and communicating with each other that magic happens. Without a team effort, sales, marketing, and product development can go south quickly.

At CGUSA we launched a new division and set up new, dedicated marketing / sales / product development teams for it that were all supported by the same CGUSA "back of house"—finance, operations, quality control, and legal. The sales and product development team consisted of longtime employees who earned promotions to this new division. Marketing was a team of three who had done great work as consultants for CGUSA. The marketing team was more senior, with successes under their belt. The sales and the production teams were just as good, with less experience, and chosen because of their alignment with the division identity, millennial / Gen Z. The group started off well, identifying the target customer, brand building, and developing products, but the second they hit marketing development, the division meetings became unbalanced, unproductive, out of harmony.

What imagery inspired followers? What words pushed sales? What messages engaged customers? Every question asked was fought over. Marketing team members met in private to gain support so others could be cornered into agreement. Resentment and frustration abounded. The signs had all been there early on, but as a part-time leader of the division, I thought those signs were just an indication that they needed time to gel. I failed to see them for what they were: efforts in silos created classic passive-aggressive behavior that morphed into overt bullying. The life was sucked out of the team, they were greatly out of balance and harmony, and eventually, the insurmountable discord killed the endeavor.

Each functional area supports and impacts the others' success or failure. As we see in the example above, a lack of alignment from the onset created dysfunction and infighting that couldn't be overcome, and the company project died. Sometimes it is the zeal for one's craft or vision that leads to leaving the rest of the team behind. Turn that zeal into a team effort, and make the magic happen.

In the next chapter, we'll focus on sales.

» **You have amazing, unintentional marketers on your team and in other departments.** Have you ever had a team member recommend a restaurant to you in a way that made you rush out and make a reservation? That's why the best first action you can take is asking your employees about your company. If they can't recommend it back to you in a way that makes you feel good, then roll up your sleeves and get to work on what you wish they had said.

» **Data, data, data.** Successful marketing can't exist without it. Collect it, sort it, measure it. How does it hold up to the ideals you have for your organization? If you fall short, gather the team, set goals, measure performance, and then get back out there and ask the questions of your staff and customers again. Wash, rinse, repeat until you have honed your company to meet your ideal message.

» **Don't hide from the issues;** see them for what they are, and adapt.

» **Bite off *only* what you can chew.** When it comes to marketing, the sky is the limit, and so are the costs. There's what you dream of doing, what you should do, and then what you can afford. Always market smart.

» **Marketing and product development suffer when sales runs the company.** Sales and product development suffer when marketing runs the company. Sales and marketing suffer when product development runs the company. *Everybody* suffers when finance or legal runs the company. Remember, it's about a team. A well-balanced, in-harmony, trusting team that celebrates each other every time a touchdown is scored! And picks each other up when we miss.

CHAPTER 3

FUNCTIONAL AREA 2: SALES

The line was already ringing on the other end. Was I really doing this? Yes. Yes, I was. I had tried everything in my bag of tricks, and still I couldn't get my retail buyer Wanda to buy into the latest sales promo, which meant I was going to achieve only 60 percent of my sales quota. I was doing her a favor anyway. I mean, her refusal to buy the product from me was a detriment to her company. I needed to take drastic measures to keep that from happening ...

"Terry here."

"Hello, Terry, this is Andrea Chuchvara with Ralph Lauren Fragrances. Do you have a minute?"

"A minute, how can I help you?"

"Well, I wanted to make sure you were aware of our fantastic Polo duffel bag promotion and the potential sales boost it would provide your store."

"You need to talk to our buyer, Wanda."

"Yes, I did, and I just felt compelled to run it by you so Robinson's wouldn't miss out on this amazing opportunity."

The pressure to win was so overwhelming at our division of L'Oréal, I crossed the respected invisible line that day. I went over the buyer's head straight to her boss. I made the sale and met my sales goals, but at what cost?

Wanda was a tough buyer and was known to make salespeople cry. I had been doing battle with her over the duffel bag promotion, but try as I might, every tactic we discussed at the Ralph Lauren sales meeting—hard data from past promotions, current sales trends versus inventory levels, and advertising dollars that I would gladly supply to support the sales—was failing. Wanda was not having any of it, and that day, in order to *win*, period, I went over her head and sold the promo to her boss. At Ralph Lauren Fragrances, winning was always the primary goal. At the next sales meeting, I would have a great story to tell, receive a bonus, and feel part of the team! That feeling of success was fleeting. What would happen the next time I saw Wanda? The fall promotion was small compared to holiday sell-in goals. I had won the battle but not the war. To win the war, I'd have to keep using my secret weapon, her boss. I was determined to make sure her boss was in our next meeting. I soon learned that although Wanda's boss might be at the meeting, I would not. While I was celebrating my win, Wanda's boss was reaching out to my *new* boss to discuss removing me from the account.

Fortunately for me, my new boss had a different winning style and gave me the opportunity to try again on another, more prestigious account. How would I rise to the occasion? More ammo, grit, and perseverance at all costs? Waging war? No, not this time. I had learned the cost of my mistakes. What I found out from the salesperson that took over for me on the "Wanda" account was that in doing what I believed was required by management—to win at all costs—I had scorched the earth there. The damage was palpable when I would meet with my colleague. She believed her difficulties were all because Wanda was tough as nails. I knew I had added fuel to the fire. Luckily, my shame was obscured by the appearance of a new boss and the promotions and account changes she made at that time.

Data, Wits, and Will

I was in sales for the Ralph Lauren fragrance division of L'Oréal, then called Cosmair. We had perfectly conceived marketing strategies, sales promotion initiatives, and valuable items to sell. At the time Ralph Lauren Fragrances ranked in the top five highest-selling brands in retail stores. But why did I always feel like I was being armed for a bloody battle rather than an engaging, productive business meeting with my buyer?

In 1989 there was no direct-to-customer internet selling. All prestige and luxury sales like this went through brick-and-mortar stores. The corporate offices for these brick-and-mortar stores had central buyers to which we sold our product. They, in turn, would distribute the goods to their hundreds of stores that would then sell to the end user in a mall environment. It still happens like this today, but now there are a greater variety of distribution channels. So off I would go to my central-office buyer's appointment, wondering, "Do I have enough ammo?" "Have I anticipated well enough the buyer's defenses?" "Am I prepared enough for the counterattacks?" And finally, "I must return victorious lest I be replaced as a frontline sales warrior."

The buyers on the other side of the table were just as well prepped: mountains of data to shoot down my push to sell in more goods to support the marketing and sales promotion initiatives; buying restrictions due to slow sell-through of past promotions or a glut of inventory; and buying dollars being allocated to competitors whose programs and products seemed better than ours. It was always a battle of data, wits, and will. Sharpen your pencils, warm up your calculator, put on your armor! Did it really have to be this way? I would soon

> **"It was always a battle of data, wits, and will ... did it really have to be this way?"**

learn that the answer to that question was a resounding no.

The summer before I crossed the line with Wanda's boss, all the salespeople from Ralph Lauren Fragrances attended a national sales conference where marketing and product development would present the strategy for fall, holiday, spring, and the following summer. It was wholesale theater at its finest. One room was decorated as a high school football game with bleachers and bright lights for Friday-night football, cheerleaders and all. It was the feeling and the experience they were planning for the end consumer to inspire them to jump up from reading the Sunday newspaper or watching television and run to the store to buy the latest promotion, a handsome Polo duffel bag to go with the purchase of a men's cologne. The next room was candelabra and crystal, tuxes and taffeta, topiary trees, ribbon, and champagne to give the feeling of a holiday party and gift exchange.

Surrounded by these fun and beautiful displays, we would learn about our budgets and sell-in requirements. We'd be provided our sell-in marketing sheet and supplies, discuss negotiating tactics, and prepare to be judged as the worthy sales warriors they wanted us to be. Here we recounted our tales of selling battles won and bonuses awarded and lamented the poor souls that couldn't hack being on the winning team. Were these meetings inspiring? Yes! Did I feel like I was on a winning team? Yes! I was a believer, and yet I could never convince myself to feel good about the culture, as I saw it, of *win* at all costs.

It was shortly after my experience with Wanda that I had my sales "aha!" moment that completely changed the way I approached sales going forward. I was speaking to one of our marketing team members in New York, letting her know I was on a new account. As I was complimenting her on the topiary, taffeta, crystal, and champagne customer-experience room from that summer, it hit me—we did not provide our buyers with a customer experience. In fact, we did not treat our buyers as the customer at all, other than giving them the occasional lunch or dinner. To both sides of the table, the customer was the consumer, the end user of the product. We were not providing *any* customer experience to our *actual* customers, the retail buyer. I talked with her about this for a while, then asked her for a big favor. She had worn a beautiful Ralph Lauren taffeta holiday gown during her summer presentation of our holiday promotion. I asked if she would lend it to me for an idea I had brewing. She was hesitant but wanted to help and sent it to Los Angeles for my idea of an experiential selling test.

My new account buyer would have an experience no other buyer in the country would. My account coordinator, Andrew, and I asked our buyer to meet us in a training room that we had transformed into a holiday party filled with chocolates, champagne, gifts (our actual products the buyer would be buying), trees, lights, and music. Andrew in his tux and I in my taffeta dress welcomed our buyer into our warm, inviting holiday home. She was surprised and delighted. We stayed in character, selling the "gifts" to her as though she was the consumer buying for her loved ones whose homes she would be entering during the holiday season, bringing gifts. We had a lovely time *and* surpassed our sales goal! It was so impactful that she asked us to replicate it at their top store that Christmas. We had a saying at our company for holiday promotions, "Stack 'em high, watch 'em fly," referring to the fragrance gift sets on all the counters in department stores. That year our buyer overachieved her goals too.

Create a culture that focuses on your actual customer: surprise and delight them! Find a way to bring celebration into the work they are doing by showing them you enjoy it too, and you both win!

Sales Culture

Sales is not always about dollars and cents. It's about relationships. Sales is not always about the point of sale. It's about getting, keeping, and growing customers. If you have a top-performing salesperson who is regularly turning over your client base (or being asked to be removed from an account), it's time to think about your sales culture. Is it productive or unproductive? Productive sales happen through caring, meaningful conversations. Anyone who has walked into a store has experienced this. The salesperson asks, "May I help you?" You reply, "No, thank you. I'm just looking." Game over. But the salesperson can't let it go, because they are there to sell, right? So they push. You resist. They push some more. You get annoyed and buy a little something just to get away. That is not a meaningful exchange that will motivate you to return to the store. A more meaningful exchange would be, "How is your shopping day going?" Whether you respond positively or negatively, the door is now open for further conversation. That's when productive selling begins. Information is exchanged, needs and wants are discovered, understanding (budget, purpose, timing) occurs, and credit cards and/or customer purchase orders appear.

Productive sales are sales that the customer desires and believes are worth the money spent. There is nothing worse than buyer's remorse. An unproductive sale that results in the customer's regret over the purchase and subsequent return of goods has a far greater negative impact on a company than the positive impact of a happy sale. Unproductive sales are the result of insufficient sales strategies coupled with sales goals that may be unachievable. Productive sales are the result of a positive customer experience. Productive sales provide your customer the solution to their problem: it makes their life easier—your job is to show them how.

After learning from my years at Ralph Lauren, I pointed out to my new team at Donna Karan that our job was to make the buyer's (our customer's) job easier, help them win, and feel good about it. The salesperson who makes their job easier is going to be the first person they turn to for help with a promotion or space on the floor that needs something amazing. I would tell my team to be ready at all times for opportunity because that prime floor space that makes money might be offered to you on the fly, and you have to be ready to fill it. You have to be ready to say, "I got you covered. Don't worry. We'll bring the team. We'll make it happen for you." That customer-centric mindset must be prevalent *throughout* the company, because remember: sales can only make these promises with product that R&D can create and operations can assemble and ship. Go team!

Selling Through

A good salesperson isn't going to *ask* the customer what they need. She's going to *tell* them what they need. A good salesperson is going to find out what is motivating her customer to buy. For example, if she is the end user shopping the cosmetics department, it may sound like this: "Oh, you have a girlfriend weekend coming up—how fun! Wouldn't it be nice if you all could enjoy the items in this amazing gift with purchase so you all have a little something special for the weekend?" This salesperson will have a meaningful conversation and learn about her customer's girlfriends while recommending other products along the way. Now, instead of walking out with just one purchase to receive the free gift promo, the customer is leaving with a whole bag of goodies. Goodies that she is going to market to her friends this weekend.

That strong salesperson is going to encourage that customer to gather everything on the counter, show her how to use the product, and boost her confidence in being able to demonstrate the product to her girlfriends. That's selling through. Now, on the back end at corporate, the data is gathered to show how big the average sale was against that gift with purchase, and that data is like gold the next time you're going to sell in your promo deal to the buyer in the corporate office. Make sure you have a way to get that feedback from your buyer. She may say, "Remember that great gift with purchase that sold through $15 million? My phone rang off the hook until we were able to build back all the baseline inventory." Armed with hard data but with the intent to celebrate the success, you can say, "That's fantastic! Congratulations! This time, instead of buying only $10 million in promotional support inventory, let's work together to capitalize on another great promotion and buy at least $15 million or, better yet, let's be aggressive this time and buy $20 million to make sure there is support inventory to do even better than the last time!" Two wins in a row! Who could say no to that?

Building Blocks to Strong Sales

Whether you are selling services, consumer packaged goods, or hard goods like cars and equipment, you must have a process for customer feedback. The same is true whether you are selling direct to the end user (B2C) or business to business (B2B). The key is to have a process for customer feedback that communicates via all channels you are selling through. Direct messaging through social media, customer service follow-up calls, online surveys: wherever the point of sale is, provide your customer the opportunity to share feedback. All that data you collect only benefits you if you analyze and use the findings to improve your customers' experience. Is your demographic living on a continuous diet of online engagement? If so, you better keep up because your once-a-week post will get squashed by the onslaught of info entering their feed. Is your demographic slow buyers who research and need more information? Then have info videos ready for them to click on.

At Cosmetic Group, Judy told me the story of landing her first multimillion-dollar order from a client. She started her day with calls to her clients, asking, "How can CGUSA make your day better today?" She did that every day for months, always getting that much closer to the sale. Al told her she was wasting her time, and he never believed she would close that deal. The lesson here is that she did close that deal by providing a direct channel for feedback, to the extreme. Every day, and no matter the answer, she put that feedback into a loop of solution and change that brought the deal closer and closer to success. We still use that concept today. Now it's mutual. Our top-to-top meetings are a two-way street of solutions and changes, pain points and joys of working together. Sharing that up- and downstream in the company helps us understand our weakness and strengths. We open ourselves to constructive criticisms and improve accordingly to make our client's day a little better. Thanks, Judy!

Whether you sell online, in brick-and-mortar stores, or through TV ads or social sales organizations, the customer experience remains critical and is always evolving—stay ahead of the curve. The customer car-buying experience ten years ago is drastically different from the customer car-buying experience today. Gone are the heydays of high-pressure salespeople, fast-talking finance managers, and the feeling of going into battle so you wouldn't be taken advantage of. Today you can buy and sell your car online with no pressure and complete transparency.

Make no assumptions. Do not assume your customer knows all the benefits of your product or service. Ask your customer questions that provide you insight as to how your product will best benefit them, and then share all the solutions your product/service will provide them. The more they see that *you* know what you are selling and how it impacts their world, the sooner they'll become a believer. A believer equals sales.

Before you have sales, you must have a product to sell. On to product development and research and development (R&D) we go.

» **Sales must be in harmony with marketing and product development.** Sales is the ambassador of the customer experience that marketing developed, the zealous believer in the items product development created, and the touchstone for change should the customer feedback be unfavorable.

» **Marketing is strategy + magic.** Sales is strategy + execution + feedback on customer interaction. All of this equals customer experience.

» **Sales is about getting, keeping, and growing your customers:** it's about relationships. Get to know your customer, and make meaningful, productive sales.

CHAPTER 4

FUNCTIONAL AREA 3: PRODUCT DEVELOPMENT AND R&D

It's the quiet before the storm of a New York City trade show. All the vendors, myself included, have returned to the floor bright and early to put the final touches on our booths that we set up the night before. Whispering voices, occasional yawns, and the aroma of coffee fill the expansive, high-ceilinged room. I stand back for one last critical look at our booth. I tweak the lipstick display and check the time. Perfect. Ten minutes until our meeting with an important global client who is hoping to get an exclusive on CGUSA's revolutionary new product that we are going to show them. I pull a sample out to do a final test. I take the cap off and … No! *No, no, no!* The tip of the eye pencil is literally crumbling in my hands! I grab another pencil—another crumbling mess. I say a prayer and reach for a third. Pieces! Little, tiny, pieces! It is then that I realize the product is absorbing the moisture floating around in this room, whose air conditioning can't keep up with the record-high humidity levels.

My mind is racing; all the effort that was put into making this product, packaging it, and getting this appointment with MAC Cosmetics—a giant in the industry. Securing them would be a real coup for CGUSA. I look up to see Judy heading my way with bright eyes and a big smile on her face, excited to sell her latest creation. This is her baby, and she can't wait to show it off. Out of the corner of my eye, I see the MAC representatives about thirty feet away, waiting for me to signal them that we're ready. I shove the pencils back in the bag and toss it under the table. It's time to punt.

When Product Development Runs the Company

When product development is in charge, steps can get missed when ideas are pushed through. The same will happen if sales runs the company or finance runs the company or operations runs the company—things will inevitably get missed, and efforts fail due to lack of harmony. This is why I will say again and again that all functional areas have to work together in balance to facilitate a company's success.

All functional areas have to work together in balance to facilitate a company's success.

This story of CGUSA's development of a revolutionary product is a perfect example of the consequences of missed steps. The steps that got missed in this scenario? Testing, testing, testing, and more testing.

Breaking into the Baked-Powder Market

It was early 2012, and CGUSA was trying to break into the baked-powder market. In cosmetics there's a particular type of product that when you combine all the ingredients, it comes out looking like a soft clay. Then you form this product into a three-dimensional shape and bake it in the oven like a cookie. Once it's baked, it has special properties that allow it to be used wet or dry. When it's dry, it's light, and when it's wet, it's more intense and vibrant. It is generally used in eyeshadows and blushes. We thought if we could mold the powder into a pencil format, shaping it like a slim lipstick, you could use it like a pencil on your eyes. It could be applied dry for a light, soft look, and it could be dipped in a little bit of water to be applied for a more intense look.

The initial phase of its development occurred before I had taken on the role of CEO. The two founders, Judy in product development and Al in operations, had been working together on this project, and they were spending some money on equipment and testing, but they were doing it in a fly-by-the-seat-of-your-pants kind of way. There was no formal structure to their R&D process and procedures. They could hardly contain their own excitement at having hit on something that could provide the marketplace with an exceptional, never-been-done-before product. And, to top it off, this would be their first prototype. In their excitement, their ability to plan for the future of this product objectively was greatly diminished.

Most of the time, in B2B, when you start to sell something, you're trying to teach your client what's different about the product and how they can talk about it to their end user in such a way that the client believes it's special or the end user believes it's special. Judy and Al, however, were talking about the technical process of getting it done. I said, "Whoa, wait, stop. You're giving our secrets away." I explained that they needed to sit down and think about whether this was a patented process or a trade secret and that we needed to make some decisions about how we wanted to treat this product.

Then the 2014 NYC trade show happened.

Punt and Recover

I've stashed the crumbling eye pencils and, with a smile on my face, give Judy a resounding "Good morning!" Judy replies, "Good morning, Andrea," and she waves the MAC reps over. I have an idea of how to flip this meeting and not show the pencils, but with no time to explain to Judy, I simply tell her that I forgot to bring the pencils. While Judy is picking her chin up off the floor in disbelief, I whisper in her ear, "We're going to talk to Estée Lauder's global supplier relations." My thought was that if we let MAC know we're meeting with their parent company, Estée Lauder, more on a global all-brand basis, it'll buy us time to address whatever had gone wrong with the pencil. MAC is owned by Estée Lauder Companies, a global powerhouse that owns many other cosmetics companies, like Clinique, Smashbox, and Too Faced. My idea was to pause the pitch and present the exclusive opportunity to the head of global supplier relations and let her meet with the brands to gain consensus for a timed launch by each brand.

The meeting, though nerve-racking, was a success, and when it was over, I came clean to Judy about the crumbling pencils. She was glad I had switched gears, and this was the opening I needed to have the difficult conversation about establishing clear R&D protocols and procedures, determining return on investment, and testing, testing, testing. Although Judy better understood now why I talked testing so much, her philosophy remained the same—get it out into the market, fix it while it's out there, and call the fixes new and improved. I explained again that you can't have a failure when you are doing a big launch with a company—if the product fails, it's done, customer confidence diminishes, and your investment is lost.

Get Ready for Tough Conversations

Not long after we returned from the trade show, a client who had previously seen one of our eye-pencil samples via one of Judy's "Bag of Tricks" secret meetings recognized that it was a unique item and wanted more information about it. This secret meeting had been right around the time that the switch in leadership was happening and I was asked to come on board as the CEO. After experiencing the stability issue at the trade show, I had to call this client and say, "I know you're interested, and yes, it is an excellent product, but we haven't industrialized it, so we have to wait." That was my way of saying we hadn't thoroughly tested it yet.

That was a tough conversation because oftentimes when you tell a client a product isn't ready or you're not willing to share information about it, they think that you're hiding something and that maybe you've found another client to give the project to. Once you've opened that gate, they're constantly questioning and waiting for the product to come out and believe that you've betrayed them when things don't materialize. Client relationships are one more reason to ensure that your product or service is truly ready—testing and strategy complete—before any potential client has so much as a sneak peek. It turned out that, through rigorous testing and regulatory investigation, we discovered that an ingredient that made the product viable would soon be restricted in Europe and had been removed, since the United

States would typically follow suit. This detail was missed before the New York show, and as a result, we had to go back to the drawing board completely.

Every company should create product development criteria, a standard that asks, Is it safe? Is it desirable? Is it profitable? Is it practical? Judy's vision for a new product started with the question, "Why hasn't anyone ever … ?" In our case the question was, "Why hasn't anyone ever tried to put baked powder into a more user-friendly pencil form?" The next step is to brainstorm and list all the reasons why somebody hasn't done it before. This process must be highly collaborative to be successful. Your product development team is the most obvious member of this collaboration since they will be tasked with figuring out how to produce the product. However, it's imperative that you also include your marketing, quality, finance, legal, operations, and sales teams. You need all functional areas involved because, no matter where you are in a functional area, you still need all those other areas to get the product to market and for it to sell once there.

Now, as you are ideating and creating your list of why-nots, you're also listening to insights from all the different functional areas, which may uncover an opportunity or a pitfall during the development process. As you go down the list of obstacles, your team can determine which ones the company can solve for and which ones it can't, and then you begin to form a picture of what is possible. Whoever initially envisioned this product sees it in its completed form. Now, through this process, the team has decluttered the vision of all its technical details so that everyone is able to envision the final product, and a plan to develop it can be mapped.

Testing, Testing, and More Testing

In cosmetics and many other industries, there are various levels of testing for consumer products. Safety is usually first. For example, is a product safe for use around the eye? Formula stability is another. Have you ever noticed how oil and water won't stay mixed together no matter how much you shake the bottle? It's like that for cosmetics too. If you try to create a formula with ingredients that don't mix, you have an unstable formula. Another example is potato chips. Have you ever reached your hand into an open bag, your mouth watering for that salty crunch, and get a soft, unsatisfying mouthful instead? The same happens in cosmetics. If materials used in the formula are water absorbent, those materials will soak moisture up from the air, just like a bag of chips left open will. Have you ever tried to refreeze melted ice cream? Yuck! Grainy, not creamy, right? So, too, with cosmetics. Imagine your body lotion is shipped from a facility in Maine to Miami during a nor'easter. It freezes on the way and then thaws sitting in the truck once it hits Miami. Without testing, you may receive a sticky oil on top of a smelly mess. If the stability of the product is not tested for under all these conditions, look out! You will have plenty of customer complaints.

Think up every conceivable scenario under which your product must perform, and test for it. Be sure to write out your testing plan, testing for each scenario separately and together. Performance under all conditions is critical. Will your product work well in conjunction with others? Can it withstand shipping and customer abuse, or are you busy selling the conditions under which it has to be used?

A word on consumer trials and focus groups. If you are Pepsi and want to test for consumer reaction to lemon flavor in the Pepsi, why not? You have the money. Most of us don't have that kind of budget.

If you are going to engage in this type of testing, be sure to set clear goals, like ease of use across all age groups, performance when applied to all skin tones, or blind trial against a competitor's product, like taking the Pepsi Challenge against Coke. Use your test data to adjust, *or* perhaps buck convention, and just believe in your vision.

A great example of bucking convention and a great lesson in visionary product development was my time at Donna Karan. We had a high-functioning team. We were in sync and getting ready to launch the body-product extensions to Donna's first fragrance, Signature. All of us were from the fragrance industry and knew how all the great fragrance brands created multimillion-dollar fragrance and body-care launches called "blockbusters." Packaging was key since all the products need to look like a "family" that belonged together with the fragrance bottle. And, of course, the scent in the body product must be exactly like the fragrance itself, no matter the density of the cream or lightness of the lotion or foaminess of the bath gel. Well, Donna rejected these proposed products, lock, stock, and barrel. What??!! They were perfect. Everyone had worked *together* to make them so. Donna wanted to buck convention and chose other shapes for the packaging, different sculptures her husband, Steven, created, and—taboo of all taboos—a different scent altogether! We were stunned. Donna would have it no other way. Wait, what happened to it being a team sport? How were we going to sell this to the retailers? Donna herself provided the vision. She wanted a body-product scent that complemented the final touch of the actual fragrance, and so was born the trend of single-note scents that dominated the industry for twenty years. Some creators have vision. If you are lucky enough to work with one, you may just need to roll with it and support the vison from all other departments.

When to Pull the Plug

Once you decide to pull the trigger on developing a product, you also must be prepared to pull the plug if necessary. Just as every company needs to establish product development criteria, the same holds true for deciding when to end development of a product. The old adage "*Can't* is not in our vocabulary" can be a dangerous one. It's true that with enough time and money, a company could make just about anything, but what will the return on investment be? There are so many pieces to consider. What's on the horizon? Where is the need? Are you filling a gap that your competitors are working on? Beta Max versus VHS and then DVD versus Blu-ray are perfect examples because those types of transformations are constantly determining whose company or idea is going to live and whose is going to die. In that scenario you must move quickly and with a finite end date. And if you don't hit the date? Then it's time to reassess and ask what's happening. Are we behind? And if we are behind, are we in the type of market where it's okay to be number two, or do we need to be number one?

New trends, changes in regulations, and even social media influencers can change the trajectory of your product's development. In the case of CGUSA and the baked-powder pencil, we were hard at work perfecting the product, and then a change in regulations prohibited us from using one of our main ingredients when selling in certain countries. We are a global company and couldn't continue on the same track once the new regulation was in place, so we headed back to R&D to figure out how to do it without that particular ingredient. These unforeseen challenges can set you back months, even years, in bringing a product to market, thus requiring you to continually reassess and ask the tough questions.

TRENDS AND INFLUENCERS

Shifting trends are not new to most industries. They are, however, more challenging to predict in the era of social media marketing. In cosmetic the trend had been to use powder products to add contouring to one's face— darker here, lighter there in order to give your face the appearance of a different shape or to accentuate certain features. Then, when a makeup artist created a YouTube video on contouring with wax-based cream colors, influencers started commenting and sharing, and overnight, customers were trading in their powders for cream-color products. At CGUSA, we supply products to some of the giants in the industries, and when trends shift, we need to shift with them. We took the contouring product that we manufactured in powder and recreated the same colors and shapes in cream form within three months—a record time, since development can take nine months to a year.

And what about reassessing production of your current goods? Once you've brought a product to market, your focus is on sales and replenishment. The product does well over time, and now you're busy securing your margins through operational excellence because you've been making it long enough that you are able to look at reducing costs. What you're not thinking about is your competitor, who is developing ways to make a product like yours, but better, right now.

That's what happens when you see an old, tried-and-true product suddenly disappear from the shelves, and you can't find it anywhere.

Somebody came in and made it better, faster, cheaper, whatever, and the original company didn't even see it coming. And that's the other part of product development—when is it *time* to reassess existing products? Say your new product is a success, and everyone's happy—development, marketing, sales, finance, operations, legal. That's great, but even before the celebration ends, it's already time to think about that product's shelf life. Is it three years? Is it ten years? If it's like the digital industry, its shelf life may be less than twelve months.

This is where your marketing and sales teams come in. Your marketing is monitoring trends, researching what's out there on the market, who your competitors are, and how your product is selling. Your sales team is out there in the trenches. They can hear what people are saying about your products and your competitor's products. Sometimes they'll come across a product that is strikingly similar to one of your products, with a slight tweak in design or function. Many companies try to lock down their great new product by patenting it. Patenting isn't always the answer, because your competitors can read your patent, and depending on how it's written, your patent may give them leeway to change a screw or the size or add some extra bell or whistle—just tweak it enough to not be identical to your product. They just made your product better because the way the patent was written allowed them to do that. Better to be looking at how to improve or

> **You may develop the most innovative product in the world, but if making it bankrupts the company, then your company is certainly out of balance.**

innovate than how to spend money defending a patent, unless, of course, your item is so unique and desired by the market that you risk everything without a patent.

Remember that as product development, you have a cost and price responsibility. You may develop the most innovative product in the world, but if making it bankrupts the company or so few people can afford it that sales would not sustain the company, then your company is certainly out of balance. Make sure your sales, finance, quality, marketing, and operations teams work with you to vet your ideas. With more great thinkers in the room, you may find many more revenue-generating ideas!

There are many conversations that need to be had with all functional areas throughout the product development process. Should we make the product, and why? How do we make the product? How much will it cost? How much will we charge? What price will the market bear for this item? How do we want to treat this product before it goes to market—patent it, make it a trade secret like the formula for Coca-Cola? How and when do we want to talk about this product even before it hits the market? Product development is a collaborative process of creating and reassessing with vision, discipline, and risk.

» **Don't jump the gun—envisioning and developing a new product is exciting, but shiny and new doesn't always spell success.** Ask the tough questions in collaboration with all your functional areas.

» **Test, test, and retest.**

» **Price right—understand your costs.** Build your price from the bottom up: cost of goods, cost of sales, overhead, product development / R&D, general and administrative costs, loss. Then, and only then, add your profit margin to the price.

» **Keep your eye on your ROI!** Continually assess the cost to go to market and know when to pull the plug if the costs are too high and your return on investment is projected to be too low.

» **Determine how to best treat your product:** Patent? Trade secret?

FUNCTIONAL AREA 4: FINANCE AND DATA ANALYSIS

//

❙❙ What are you doing back here?" Al growled at me.

"I'm investigating," I replied, keeping my eyes glued to the notebook in my hand.

"Investigating? Investigating what?"

"Investigating where the money is going."

"It's going into making and shipping the products, that's where it's going."

"Yes, but we need to find ways to keep less of it from going." That's when I put my pencil down and looked him in the eye. Taking a deep breath, I said, "You know that huge L'Oréal project that you landed?" His eyes narrowed and he gave the slightest of nods. "Well, we're losing five cents every single time we make a piece."

"The hell we are!" Al's modus operandi when challenged was to get loud and angry, and true to form, that's what he proceeded to do.

I cut him off as quickly as possible, instructing him to take a good look at the line with me. I grabbed my stopwatch and pointed to the assembly line, with Al still yelling and screaming. We started running takt time (in manufacturing, your takt time is the assembly duration of one unit required to meet the shift demand) to make sure that what was coming off the line was what was supposed to be coming off the line in the allotted time. It was clear that there were unforeseen extra steps that weren't being accounted for and therefore not included in the pricing.

"This is where too much of the money is going," I said, pointing to the line. He didn't want to believe it, but then again, he never wanted to believe he was wrong or had missed something.

His eyes mere slits and his face flaming red, he crooked a finger at me and said, "Come with me." So we walked back toward the office, and he whipped around, jerking open the office door that takes you out into the factory. Pointing to the floor, he snarled, "You see this yellow line?"

I looked down at the yellow demarcation that signals you're crossing over onto the manufacturing floor.

"Do. Not. Cross. This. Line." Impossibly, his face had grown redder, and he was nearly trembling with rage.

I looked at him, a friendly smile on my face, lifted my foot, and, as if the floor on the other side of the yellow line was a warm bath just waiting for me, I gently dipped my toe to the other side of the line. "You mean like this?" I asked calmly, still smiling.

Well, he let out a big old belly laugh, and soon we were both laughing. My silliness didn't solve the problem, but it did at least dissolve the tension in that moment, and it allowed me to get back to the task at hand—following the money.

Finance Is a Contact Sport

Finance is often an underutilized resource. Everything eventually rolls to finance. Every action the company takes and every result of those actions show up in—you got it—finance. I like to think of finance as the contact sport of the functional areas. I don't mean contact as in "Let me grab the ball and push everybody out of my way." I mean contact as in balls are being lobbed at finance all the time from every department. Whether it's a sales order that has incorrect pricing, purchase orders from engineering that don't have the proper general ledger code assigned to them, expenses out of control in R&D, or labor costs out of control in operations, it all flows back to finance. It's what you do with that constant barrage of information that determines how finance helps the organization become its best self. If your finance person is simply a recorder of numbers who spits out a profit and loss statement and a balance sheet, your company will not be set up for success. Why? Because the numbers need to be analyzed, and that is where the critical position of cost accountant comes in. The cost accountant does most of the financial analysis. If you don't have a cost accountant, your controller needs to be versed in cost accounting. They need to understand it because it is through their diligent analysis that irregularities will be caught early and adjusted for before too much cash has blown out the door.

Follow the Money

You're ready to dig into finance—but where do you begin? Surprisingly, not sitting in the finance office. You begin asking questions in all the other departments. You go to quality control and ask what their expenses are on a daily, weekly, and monthly basis. You go to product and development and see what they're working on. You check the line, like I did with Al. You make contact with every functional area to see what their costs are and where the costs are coming from, because remember, it all funnels back to finance, and if finance doesn't understand the hows and whys, they won't be able to decipher the cause of variances—variances that could lead to costly mistakes.

> **You can have a fantastic product, an abundance of orders, great on-time shipping stats, and happy customers and still not make any money.**

You can have a fantastic product, an abundance of orders, great on-time shipping stats, and happy customers and still not make any money.

Let's start with pricing, because if that's not set right, increasing your sales will not increase your profits.

The L'Oréal product that we were losing five cents per piece on had an abundance of orders and shipped on time, and our customer was ecstatic, but not only were we not making a profit, we were literally losing money. In this scenario we saw where the problem was—operations. It took a few arm wrestling sessions with Al for me to get him to accept what had gone wrong and to let me fix it, but it's the perfect example of the need for collaboration and communication between functional areas. When finance is providing operations financial reports on a weekly basis and questioning any variances, problems can be quickly solved or avoided altogether.

If the money is not being lost in operations, maybe the trail will lead to R&D. At CGUSA, we use a lot of raw materials to make our products, and sometimes those materials change for a variety of reasons. Now, if R&D doesn't tell finance that a new material is coming in and that they are shelving the old material and using the new material, finance continues to use the standard cost. Suddenly they notice a variance. If you have the right finance person, they're going to ask why there is a variance. They're going to do a bit of digging and connect it to R&D. This is where CAPA (corrective action, preventative action) plays an important role. That is what quality control uses as the process to make sure that they can show the corrective action for whatever the FDA or an auditor from any party came in and found as what is called an observation (anything they would like to see improved upon). In the materials scenario, finance will get to the root cause of what happened and then gather the appropriate players, whether it's inventory control, supply chain, R&D, quality, whoever it is, and ask how we are going to fix this and how we prevent it from happening in the future. CAPAs are the quality mechanism for all departments to ensure the problem is identified, solved, and prevented from happening again.

A solution could be to have all-new raw materials go through the vice president of R&D first. The vice president of R&D talks with inventory control to explain the material, the generic names it may go by, and trade names of products that are similar, and then asks how much of the material is already in stock. A form is created that all involved parties add information to, which may include R&D, quality control, regulatory, finance, purchasing, marketing, and sales, and then a final sign-off by the owner or CEO. Now we've come up with a solution to prevent new raw materials from coming in without everybody knowing about it. Every part of this process impacts pricing—does the new material cost more or less, is the old material now a loss, will the new formula take more labor and time to create?

When regulations changed and we had to change one of our raw materials, I was able to call our customers and tell them that the new material we now had to use was more expensive and that we had to adjust the price accordingly. Customers understand price increases.

They don't like them, but they understand that costs change. Now, if the change in raw material hadn't been communicated across the board and finance wasn't reconciling every day, it could have been several months and a lot of lost profits before someone figured it out. Sometimes loss is hidden, but more often than not, it's a bunch of tiny little losses that all add up because no one is paying attention.

The Hub

Finance is the hub of the company. A hub with a big picture view and the ability to zero in on every detail. Finance knows your labor, inventory, equipment—if your company buys, stores, uses, pays, or sells it, finance knows about it. Choose your finance leadership carefully—someone who understands that their role is to be supportive and collaborative with all the functional areas, a servant leader—then let them do their job. Start by asking them to weigh in on what are they seeing—trends, year-over-year costs versus sales, inventory growth rate, purchase price creep. Boo! Did I scare you? Finance can show you where the bogeyman is and shine a light in the darker corners of your organization so you and your team know what needs to be fixed.

Every department has the potential to get stuck in the weeds and forget to come up for air. Too many times I've seen our chemists go to a presentation from a raw material manufacturer and get all googly-eyed at the new material and all they can formulate and create with it and immediately say, "Yes, we need this!" And in the blink of an eye, another material is delivered to the warehouse. The right finance person is going to have eyes on the big picture and see, wow, we've got four raw materials that are almost identical. They can then go to R&D and map a plan to target the best and most cost-effective material to keep in inventory and a plan to use up or get rid of the too-similar ones that will no longer be used.

Finance can do the same thing for operations when they see labor overages, for sales and marketing when pricing isn't lining up, etc. Sometimes a department head may be so overwhelmed with projects that they spend little time looking for ways to save money, thinking instead that their time should be spent *making* more money. While on the surface this may be true, there are opportunities in all departments to save. Take sales, marketing, and quality, for example. These departments often enter into contracts with clients and vendors that, if read through carefully (my favorite way is out loud, no matter the length), reveal areas of opportunity that a cursory review would never illuminate. Just delineating which party is responsible for what can save time and money down the road, when the contract is in full swing. Renegotiating the contract after unforeseen difficulties, while not as effective, can prove useful in preventing loss. In operations we often get the "Well, this is the way we have always done it" reply when we look deeper into cost saving processes.

Finance can see the results from operation's efforts. They may not know *how* or *why* something is costing more than it should, but they can dig in and find out via question and live observation. Now, if your finance leader doesn't have the right temperament, the other departments are going to feel like they report to finance and view finance as someone who is always looking over their shoulder—choose wisely.

Data In, Data Out—What Does It All Mean?

Your enterprise resource planning (ERP) system is the brain of your organization. Every department inputs data into it: quality control, R&D, sales, operations—everyone. It's great having all this information in one system, but simply collecting the data is not enough. Oftentimes, departments are inputting data and not exporting and analyzing the data to understand what they are doing and how they are performing. Part of the problem is that ERP systems don't always come with enough reporting abilities customized to your industry. So unless you know what you're trying to get out of it, you won't be able to tell the person who's going to create your report how to create it. You could spend $15,000 creating one report only to realize that that wasn't exactly the information that you needed. That's why having a team member that knows Access and having Excel wizards on your team will save you time and money. These team members are the great equalizer for all ERP systems. You must have people with these skills because if you can't extract the data that you want in the way you want in order to glean the information that's going to help you, your ERP system is just a reporting vehicle that is not helping you do anything but collect the data.

If you're not asking questions, you can't identify or fix your problems.

Now, if you can export information that tells you how many of a particular item you made last year and how many ran at the right rate and how many didn't run at the right rate, you begin to see why that item didn't make the money it was forecast to. I'm always curious, which means I'm always asking questions. If you're not asking questions, you can't identify or fix your problems. I'm always going to finance and asking questions like, "You know what? I was really thinking about this product that should have made more money, and I need to see the full picture. Can you pull the last six runs of the product, all the work orders, all the pricing, and all the labor costs and see how we can put all that data together?"

Once I see the data, I can begin to visualize how all the pieces need to be formulated in a spreadsheet. Then your Excel wizard, who is visualizing this grand spreadsheet with you, works it all out. If that person tells you they will have it to you in a week or it will take them a month, you've got the wrong wizard. Your wizard should know how to configure what you are looking for in a day or less. Now, it may not be beautiful, it may not be perfect, but they've created the shell that contains all the information, and they've written some formulas and started to glean some useful numbers. The Holy Grail of data analysis is a flexible ERP system that provides business intelligence (BI, or a fancy way of finance saying, "We have thought through and provided all the reports you need, until you don't"). You know your unique needs. Find a wizard, no matter how good your ERP.

Once I begin to see and understand the variances, it's time to gather more information and share it with all functional areas. I call all the department heads in for a meeting, show them what's happening and why and how we missed our mark, and then, together, we begin to create solutions. Now, the next time we make this product or a similar product, we have a template that avoids the pitfalls and keeps us on the right trajectory.

Everything Must Balance

Your balance sheet reflects the health of your company. It tells you how much inventory you have versus cash, how much debt versus assets, and how those numbers compare to the same time last year. Surprisingly, a lot of people don't think that's important, but it is critically important. Your balance sheet will prompt you to ask the necessary questions. How much did our sales increase really cost us? What was the profitability on the profit and loss sheet, and how did it affect my balance sheet? If those numbers don't gel, you have a whole new set of questions that need to be asked. What's happening here? Why is my inventory growing faster than what my sales increase should call for? Why have sales skyrocketed but cash decreased? Where is all the cash being spent?

Finance can dig deeper into the numbers to answer those questions because they are in constant contact with the people who are spending the money. Is it in labor, inventory, general and administrative costs like rent, capital expenditures? Is an owner removing too much cash from the company? Or is it an uptick in payroll? Finance can't tell your departments what not to spend, but they can tell them what they are spending and how it's impacting the company's bottom line. I'm often asked, "When do you know that a company is healthy?" And I say, "When they have a lot of cash in the bank, capital investments align with revenue growth, and assets outweigh liabilities due to shareholder equity growth pattern."

It's a pretty simple equation, but getting there isn't easy. You need to arm your people with information, and finance is the team to do that. Yes, finance is going to show how much money they are spending, which is something not everyone wants to hear, but they are also going to be able to show income and profit, or lack thereof, based on spending practices. One way or another, the company's income is tied to every employee's income, right? If you share financials with your department heads and show them how to read them and what to look at, they'll understand the power they have to impact the bottom line. And if salary increases and bonuses are directly tied to the bottom line, you have buy-in and personal impact—now, instead of your department heads avoiding finance, they're knocking on their door, asking where their reports are.

» **If your finance department is just a group that receives payments, pays bills, counts inventory, and reports outcome—change it now!** The finance team is your best resource for ensuring that sales are as profitable as possible.

» **Analyze your variance reports** *every day,* **not at month end.**

» **The finance team are your friends!** They can help you find the hidden losses. If your company is leaking profit and you are plugging the leaks with sales, you're going to sink; it's just a matter of time. Quick increases in sales only serve to hide the real issues. Find the leaks and seal them, *now*!

» **Hold CAPA meetings weekly and move swiftly to test the CAPA to make sure it doesn't cause other issues downstream.**

» **Microsoft Access and Excel are the great equalizers of all ERP systems.** If you can't afford custom report writing, spend the time to build it in Excel through data gathered via Access. Cost accountants and controllers are usually wizards with these programs.

CHAPTER 6

FUNCTIONAL AREA 5: OPERATIONS, INVENTORY, AND SUPPLY CHAIN

One by one, forty-five employees were called into human resources, issued termination packages, and ushered out the door by security. Forty-five individuals terminated in one morning. What led to this devastating moment took months to build up, of course, but by the time I realized the problem and its trajectory, the damage was done, and layoffs were the only way to right the ship. All this in the middle of what would be a stellar revenue year. Yep, we were having a stellar year—in the end, we grew revenue to an increase of 40 percent over the previous year. Try justifying a huge cut in your workforce in the middle of your "best" year to date.

Do you remember when I said, "You can have a fantastic product, an abundance of orders, great on-time shipping stats and happy customers and still not make money"? I'm going to add "a huge increase in revenue" to that list … and still not make money. You can increase revenue 500 percent, but if your profit margin is moving in the opposite direction at a faster pace, you won't make money. Here's what led CGUSA down that path in 2016.

Shrinking Margins

I'm going to make a confession. As we entered 2016, I was tired. It had been three years of battle after battle after battle to grow this organization, redirect the culture, revive its reputation, and make it profitable. I was worn out. This, in hindsight, resulted in leadership missteps on my part. That year I hired a new vice president of operations, an individual with better operational skills than I had, and I was so relieved to have someone strong in charge that I essentially tossed him the keys and, for the first time in three years, took a rest in the back seat, focusing on R&D.

In 2014 our sales team had a record year. So in 2015 the revenue from those contracts began, and then in 2016 the resulting surge in growth occurred. Our sales director moved to a new job in 2016, and our founder Judy stepped into the sales role while we looked for that replacement. We had also just lost our R&D director to a medical issue, so during the hunt for a replacement, I moved my office location to R&D to lend support to the team. It was perfect timing: Judy in sales, Julio in operations, and me in R&D. What could go wrong? My mistake was not keeping the pedal to the metal, not shifting to intense operations analysis and continuous improvement while giving Julio operations execution, and not quickly hiring my leadership team in sales and R&D. I had made the classic mistake of working *in* the business, not *on* the business.

This is when the new vice president of operations began. Julio's first task became the management of our incredible surge in growth. What we didn't understand well enough at the time was how to uncover the root cause of our financial variances. Remember that finance is the hub. If there is something wrong, finance generally notices the impact first. We began tracking our variances in 2015, but we weren't experienced enough with it yet to figure out what was causing them. As I was watching our delivery on the sales growth, we were still dropping a good amount of profitability to the bottom line. With only a few months of history on the financial variances, it seemed logical that with a big revenue surge came increased variances and certain inefficiencies. So I wasn't alarmed, at first. The variances at that point weren't huge—they looked manageable. I felt proud that we had gotten to this great place of growth and that we were going to have a stellar year. However, we should have reviewed labor, overhead, and cost variances every day. Working *in* the business, I didn't see the problem coming.

Our VP of ops was doing great work, ensuring on-time delivery, meeting our quality standards, and producing it at the right cost. Wait, what? Not at the right cost? Because the surge was coming so fast and furiously, toward the end of the year, in order to continue to do the first two things well, he had to expand the more costly night shift. He began hiring new positions for both day and night in order to accommodate for the fast growth. And while the revenue trajectory had been absorbing these extra costs, at this point I could see the profit line start to decline.

During this stellar revenue year in 2016, I had stationed myself in R&D to support and guide the team. I implemented tracking dashboards created for R&D and product development. The dashboard allowed us to see what was going to be coming out of the lab and turned into a purchase order. It tracked every single project that we had, and it tracked its value to us. To give an example, our product development team member might say they were working on a lipstick and that one lipstick was going to sell for $1.50. The client had the potential to order a hundred thousand pieces of ten shades of lipstick, so that lab project would be a potential order six to nine months from now worth $1.5 million in revenue.

With that lipstick project in the lab in January, I could see that we had the potential to ship $1.5 million for that one project in September. Now I had a line of sight for the future. While we were trying to manage our growth, fighting to hold on to, let alone increase, profit, I realized something was wrong. What we were tracking as potential shipments for the following year, based on R&D projects in the lab, was not even close to what we would be shipping in the current year. So in August I realized that we were going to have a dive in revenue in the coming year. Judy, our creative director, was spread too thin running sales, and I lost focus working in R&D. Quickly filling the two vacant positions early in the year would have solved for this. Back into the front seat I went!

When I saw we were going to hit a wall and profits weren't growing, we began to analyze the costs from a different perspective. What if we had these same costs with lower revenue? It was your classic grow-too-fast scenario without a handle on cost impact. Because there was so much work to be done, we were throwing people at the problem so we could deliver on time. Of course, that meant our manufacturing overhead was also growing, something the price of the finished products hadn't been adjusted for. But when you're in the weeds, trying to make it happen and trying to support all your departments, you just don't always see it. Working closely with finance, we identified that cost variances were also creeping up. New staff that were rushed in to help fulfill the sales surge were not experienced, creating inefficiencies in many departments. The result: Higher cost and lower productivity to deliver a revenue surge. If you don't fix it, that spells disaster! Fortunately, I had time to understand what needed to be done in order to right the ship as we headed into the new year. Unfortunately, the fix was an incredibly painful one.

Continuous Improvement

In the midst of uncovering the coming issue and figuring out how we could fix it, I got a call from my top recruiter, who told me she had this client who was smart, data oriented, fast, and creative, who didn't fit the normal corporate mold. She thought of me immediately because she believed her client was the perfect fit for my style and company culture, but she didn't know where she could fit in our organization. At the time I was in survival mode, figuring out how we were going to bounce off the wall we were about to hit and still land on our feet, but I agreed to meet her, knowing there certainly was no way I could hire her now. I met with Megan on a Saturday, and at the conclusion of the interview, six hours later, I hired her. She was a chemical engineer with an impressive array of skills, experience, and natural abilities. I wasn't sure what her role would be, but I knew that somehow, she would be great for the future of our company. I kept mulling over how Megan's skills and our needs could mesh, and in two weeks' time, our new position, continuous

> **I believe in enlisting amazing people who can run circles around me, and it's my job to figure out where those circles need to be run, provide guide rails, and help facilitate the success of what they are doing.**

improvement leader, was born. I knew that Megan could help me work *on* the business rather than *in* it. She would help us analyze what was happening and figure out how we could do it better, reduce costs, and gain efficiencies. She became the boots-on-the-ground tactician for every department.

I've never been one to think I had all the answers. I believe in enlisting amazing people who can run circles around me, and it's my job to figure out where those circles need to be run, provide guide rails, and help facilitate the success of what they are doing.

I had just had turnover in R&D and was looking for a new department head. R&D is the heart of the company. If you don't have a head of R&D, who is going to guide the innovation and manage R&D operations? So I sent Megan to work with them when she first came on board. She would determine how to organize the workflow to ease the way for the additional projects we would need to bring in to shore up next year while I looked for R&D's new department head and Julio worked overtime to keep up with the demand. Now September was approaching, and I had to make a decision on how to right the ship before our fiscal year ended in January. In September we filled the R&D department head position, and Megan began to wrap up her work in that department. R&D got busy working on trade show projects to increase sales for next year, and I sent Megan to operations to begin investigating where we could reduce costs and gain efficiencies while still fulfilling the incredible sales surge we were experiencing, shipping out almost double the amount of product we had shipped the year before, on time.

Megan quickly found areas that could move the needle to save costs. She figured out that our powder-pressing process was affecting our bottom line. Pressing the powder into the compact requires a lot of pressure, which is automated. The placing of the powder into the pan before pressing is done semimanually. If you put in too much powder, you're going to overfill it. If you put in too little powder, the customer is going to notice and be dissatisfied. Quality control is there to make sure it looks properly filled, and from a visual standpoint, all did look well. Megan figured out that, depending on who the operator was and how they were setting up the machine, they were overfilling, but not to the detriment of visual or performance quality. But if you price to put two grams in and you put two and a half grams in millions upon millions of pieces, it will quickly cause a cost variance and be a detriment to your bottom line. This was one of the variances that finance saw, but it wasn't until we committed to a continuous improvement leader that we—or shall I say she—found the root cause. We immediately began implementing changes to correct for that. I forecasted how this correction would impact the bottom line. While it would help us next year, it wasn't going to be nearly enough for CGUSA to turn the required profit. What we were facing was a $10 million increase in revenue over the previous year but a significant decrease in profit percentage. A classic sign of growing too quickly and not managing it well.

The beauty of hiring Megan in the face of a coming downturn was that it allowed us to be laser focused on working *on* the company while Julio and I continued working *in* the company to deliver our biggest year to date. We had to find more savings, and fast. We had October, November, December, and January to execute on positioning the company for the impact of the coming down year. I knew it was something that couldn't be done on my own, so I gathered the team, data from finance, savings from Megan's work, and ideas from all department heads on a last-ditch effort to save those forty-five jobs, but it was clear there was no choice but to lay off these team members. Now, could we have kept all these employees and stayed afloat in a profitless, oversized ship in the coming year with the plan to rebound the next year? Quite possibly. Would the board of directors have agreed to that? With no extenuating circumstances, like a recession or a pandemic, not a chance. It was clear this was a management issue.

Don't Forget to Get Lean

We learned from the problem in 2016. After the layoffs we continued to execute on cost savings and efficiency and perform well. We brought in temporary workers to fill the lines during surges, and we managed to maintain EBITDA (earnings before interest, taxes, depreciation, and amortization) level with the prior year and realize an increase in profit, though razor thin over the prior year. We also dug deep into all aspects of production to identify and solve for inefficiencies. Julio came from a different industry and had to adapt to a new approach required then at CGUSA. As a result we were late in watching the line closely enough. Let's say, for example, that line number one ended at noon. Instead of sending all those people home and paying them for the six hours worked, supervisors didn't want to send them home without eight hours, so they kept them for an extra two and put them onto another line. All that did was increase the cost of the line that those extra people were put on. In Julio's previous company, that was unheard of, so not on his radar here, nor mine, for that matter.

Now, if adding people made that line more efficient and you could reduce the amount of time it took to make the required units per minute and improve your percentage of output versus price, that would be fine, but who's watching that? Who's making sure that happens? Nobody was. We were running as fast as we could to service the sales growth. It seems logical that adding more people would decrease your takt time, but that's not always the reality. I asked Megan to observe and study all of this. We implemented a program where we would gather and go lean out a line. All of us—finance, R&D, sales, Julio, and me—would go to the line, observe, and sometimes jump in, and see what wasn't working efficiently.

It might be that there were thirty people on the line, but we had only priced with twenty-five—Why were the extra five people there? We'd pull out the stopwatch and compare against the rate that was costed for versus actual. In this process one of the department heads might see how the line could be more efficient if we folded a unit carton differently or that switching a person on the line to a different section might improve the bottleneck that was happening. We had been out of balance in many areas, costing us the profits we should have had.

You must constantly go lean with your line—whatever that line may be. For manufacturing, it's production line performance versus price. For the transportation industry, it's scheduling, dispatch, and routing processes. For consumer brands, it's sales velocity. Brands need to know how many units of which items are selling per day. For a brand, marketing and sales promotion increase sales velocity, but at what cost? Are they out of balance? Are there too many promotions propping up sales? Is the cost of goods too high, limiting cash flow to spend on marketing and sales promotion? Some call these KPIs (key performance indicators). For online, sales conversion rate and average order value versus the acquisition cost are the metrics. Analyze what your business needs to get lean, and do it regularly.

Guess what else you must do? Collect and share the data from the lean analysis. We developed an efficiency report to show how we were performing on each line, and the reports were shared with the leads. Operations would report what they were making and how many pieces were to be made. Say they made eight thousand pieces against a goal of eight thousand, and everybody would be thrilled, but now, with the report, we learned that it took them two hours longer to make those eight thousand pieces than it was supposed to. We began adding the percent of efficiency against price, and that changed the trajectory of the team meetings. It was tough on the morale of the people working on the line because now they were seeing that they were not getting the efficiency required.

When it started to turn into excuses, we would work to solve for all these things. It was at this point that we realized we needed operations to have a seat at the table during initial concept meetings.

> **Too often we treat operations like the last line of defense. In reality they are the first line of defense.**

Too often we treat operations like the last line of defense. In reality they are the first line of defense. They are the realists at the table. They are the boots on the ground who make it on time, with top quality, and at the right cost. The rest of us are the sparkle that make it all look like magic to the customer.

We needed operations there to be able to say, "If you want me to make that, I'm going to need X, Y, and Z." Operations would take sample product boxes and fold them to confirm how much time it took. If the assumption was that it was going to take three seconds to fold that box but the box folds more like origami and it actually takes thirty seconds, operations must be there to tell you that and determine how many people are needed to make it at a particular rate. It's not just in manufacturing that operation needs a seat at the table. When I was working for Donna Karan, we would sit with our operations counterpart and ask why we were always out of stock on this product, and then operations might say that they had a supply chain issue that they could use some help with. Without ongoing communication, these issues don't get resolved for months because every department wants to take care of what they perceive to be their own problem. Month one goes by, and they're trying to take care of the problem. Month two goes by, they're still trying to take care of the problem. Month three goes by, and oops, we're out of stock.

Imagine you're out of your hero product and you can't figure out why this keeps happening. Maybe marketing ran a promotion on that product, and it sold out. Marketing is happy: their promotion worked. Sales is in a panic because they've committed to *x* number of that product to other clients and want to know why operations doesn't have the product for them. Operations is ready to throw their hands up because no one told them about the marketing promotion that was going to deplete their stock, and now it's going to take twelve weeks to replenish it. This is why everyone needs to be at the table—you must function in collaboration with all departments.

The bottom line in operations is to discover all the variables that affect profit for your unique business and analyze them, solve for them, correct the process, and gain more profit. What to look for? The various types of business have—you guessed it—different data-point needs for analysis. Cost of acquiring new customers, repeat sales timeline, size of initial and repeat sales, return on investment, sell-through percentage on a promotion period, sales velocity versus replenishment lead time plus in-stock inventory. These are concerns of a sale to the end user of consumer packaged goods. For the manufacturer of those goods, other data points need analysis. Raw material lead time, production timeline, efficiency of production versus how priced. Production accuracy versus plan and price. Once CGUSA started working together in all departments, the harmony and balance were palpable. We were back on track and delivered better profits during that "down" year than any year before. It's time to dig into your business's unique variables that are affecting your profit margin. The key is to include the voice, perspective, ideas, and knowledge of all your departments.

» **Be curious.** Investigate, test, validate theories, plan, then execute the improvement.

» **Operations must have a seat at the concept table.** Though we often treat them like the last line of defense, they are the first line of defense.

» **There is no better dollar spent than on continuous improvement.**

» **Never take a ride in the back seat.** You know when you are doing it. Take a well-deserved vacation for that, then get back up front and work *on* your business.

» **Never give up.** There is always a way forward—painful at times, but a way forward.

CHAPTER 7

FUNCTIONAL AREA 6: PEOPLE AND CULTURE

A l's voice was booming at the other end of the warehouse. "What do you mean you're not done? I told the client they could have it today!" Heads were down, and everyone's hands began moving even faster.

I was working on a production line as part of my own type of orientation as a consultant for Al and Judy. As I looked around to check why Al was shouting somewhere else in the factory, I heard our quality control lead ask, "What are you doing?"

"I'm putting labels on this product," I said, sneaking a peek at the other workers on the line with us. All heads were down. No one dared look up, let alone smile.

"Pay attention," she snapped. "You're too busy looking around instead of focusing on what you're doing. Your labels are all crooked."

"Sorry," I mumbled and bowed my head like everyone else.

"You need to go to another part of the line. I can't have you messing up those labels and causing us to take longer to fix your work." She gave a furtive glance in the direction of Al's voice. I was dumbfounded.

"Okay," I said, stepping away and looking for the production supervisor to reassign me. Carmelita stepped into my spot to keep the line going while waiting for my replacement.

I would come to learn that Carmelita was one of our best quality control personnel. She cared. True, she didn't yet have the soft skills needed to treat line employees with care—she had grown up in the world according to Al—but she was the most caring in terms of product quality. She would learn the next day that I was the new consultant to her CEO, Al, and boy, did that make her angry. Angry that I had Al's ear and, as a result, she might get into trouble. In fairness to Carmelita, she was simply fitting in with the culture of fear and intimidation that Al had fostered for years—a culture that I knew needed to change. And to accomplish that, I would pull from the culture dynamics I learned years earlier at Donna Karan.

Cancun, Anyone?

One of the first things Donna Karan did with her newly assembled leadership team of what was to be her new beauty division was connect us with a team-building and leadership organization and then fly us all to Cancun to focus solely on working on our team and leadership skills. A little different from Al's CGUSA culture, right? But important to note, Donna's culture was also extremely different from those from which her new leadership team came.

In the start-up phase of this new division, there were no systems in place, and only a handful of us were brought in to begin building them. Donna's husband, Steven Weiss, is the one who recruited and hired all of us, and he recruited us from companies who would be Donna Karan's beauty-division competitors. The team she sent to Cancun consisted of a group of six female senior-level leaders in our thirties and forties. We all came from different company cultures with one similarity: they were traditional 1980s and '90s cultures. They were political or fear based with a common theme that their way was the best and that you can't trust anyone. This was the early 1990s, and Donna was a true visionary at that time. Not just in product development but in culture development.

When we arrived at Donna Karan Beauty Company to try and build this organization, Donna understood that her team needed to gel and work together in harmony if this was going to be a success. She also understood that, based on the cultures from which we came, that wasn't going to happen without help. That's when she brought in Judy Glaser, executive coaching and management consultant. Judy began attending our management meetings and engaging with us. Initially, I thought she was a psychiatrist or psychologist because she was interacting with us in a counseling sort of way. Of course, in the beginning we all rolled our eyes at each other like, Are you kidding? We're going to do this?

Almost all of us had sales or marketing backgrounds, so we understood how to turn information we received into soundbites that would lead people toward trust in a product or company message, but we needed to learn to trust one another. In this dynamic with Judy Glaser, we were retaught how to have effective conversations that engendered clear understanding and trust. We were asked to bring our feelings into work situations and use her special art of conversation to address our emotional reactions to receiving information from one another, and then, by echoing back that information with each other, we learned to trust and become a more effective leadership team. We were essentially selling each other on this process. In the end it was extremely liberating and effective because she broke down the barriers, enabled us to remove the protective armor we acquired in our past work environments, and provided us a path toward working in a kind, thoughtful way that was company approved.

Building the Donna Karan company strategy from the bottom up on a tight budget required a lot of creativity on our part, which requires a lot of communication and teamwork. We had such a great time in Cancun, and we were so close by the time we returned home that we decided that for our planning meetings, for which we had to gather in New York, instead of each of us taking a separate hotel room, we would pool our budgets and stay at the penthouse (less costly once you did the math) of the Morgan in New York and have a slumber/ work party. We ate, drank, slept, and worked Donna Karan Beauty Company in that penthouse until we came up with our strategic plan together. I think that was the proof that the process worked: we were thoroughly enjoying the work and the relationships we were forming; trusting each other with our fears, shortfalls, and feelings; and relying on each other for our unique talents.

The most important piece I learned and take with me to every company that I'm part of is communicating with feedback. I think of it like harmonizing understanding. For example, I say something to you, you receive it, and you may respond with, "Wow, you know what? That made me feel small," or "That made me feel like you don't trust me," or "That sounds impossible." You basically respond with how the statement made you think about the information or how the way it was said made you feel, whatever that may be. Now I have the opportunity to say, "I'm sorry. I didn't realize that I said it that way. That's not how I meant it. I meant this." Or I can say, "How about I explain it a different way?" You can, in turn, repeat back what you now understand me to mean. The loop continues until there is harmony in thoughts and feelings. Why is this feedback loop critical? Because people feel what *they hear* and understand what *they hear* but often not what *you said* or how you intended to say it. This type of communication technique allows the speaker to know that you understood them the way they intended to be understood and facilitates empathy, which is essential to strong partnerships and productive, effective outcomes.

We also learned that it was okay to talk about our personal life at work. Today many companies would still frown upon that; back in the 1990s, it was definitely taboo. But as I said, Donna was a visionary, and she made sure we understood, through Judy Glaser's help, that our interactions at work were impacted by what was happening in our personal lives, so why deny it? There are some things that happen in life that you just can't "check at the door" every time. So if somebody was snappy with us, we now had permission to say, "Hey, why are you snapping at me? That makes me feel bad."

Empathy ... is essential to strong partnerships and productive, effective outcomes.

The person may not even realize how they sound, and they apologize and start to talk about why they are on edge. Maybe they are taking care of a parent with dementia or thinking about separating from their partner. It could be any number of things, but at least now it's out in the open and they recognize how it's impacting their communication with others. It also provides the other person an opportunity to empathize and extend a hand. It reaffirms the partnership and defuses the tension so that you can both get back to work.

This communication style is also helpful when managing a team. We've all been there. A request comes through from your boss, who asks in an offhand way for the work to be done by the next day. What the boss is unaware of is that for that to happen, you need to pull an all-nighter, rearrange your personal life, and pressure a couple of colleagues to get you some data by the end of the day. Not impossible, but tense, stressful, and exhausting if all one's other obligations, personal and professional, are to be met. Having had a lot to juggle myself, both professionally and personally, I now use one-on-one meetings using the communication style I learned at Donna Karan to get to know my team and ask for their input on assignments in terms of timing and make sure to clear or reassign work that isn't the immediate priority. It's really about helping the team succeed, not loading their plate with so much work they couldn't possibly sustain the load.

The positive culture at Donna Karan was successful because the head of the company embraced it and wanted it to work. If the ultimate decision maker doesn't see the need to change or prefers a negative culture, it is nearly impossible to change it. You can make it happen, but it's incredibly hard, and you must first gain support among a certain level of peers in order to begin to make the shift.

On the Line Again

After my interaction with Carmelita, I began walking the floor every day and saying, "Hello," "Good morning," and "How are you today?" to everyone. People just want to know that you care about them and are there to help them. This is such a simple thing to do and yet so rarely put into practice. Sometimes I would jump on the line with them. Now, when you're on the production line, you can't stop production to have a conversation. I learned that quickly. What you have to do is scooch yourself into the line and start folding boxes with them and just say, "How's it going?" I don't mean a superficial "How are you?" with the expectation of a standard response; I mean asking, "How's the line going? Is there anything we can do to improve it?" Or "Just wanted to check in to see if you are getting enough breaks." By doing that, you gradually build up a rapport and relationship. By the time I actually became CEO, most everyone in the company was accustomed to my check-in chats. Later they would experience how something so simple as exemplifying kindness could change the way they thought about working at CGUSA.

Building caring relationships and promoting open dialogue is simply the right thing to do when working with people. The benefits are a happier and more productive workforce and zero employee lawsuits. People and culture are critical for ensuring that the company doesn't get sued by its own people. Early on, when I was the primary people-and-culture point person, we had potential for a discrimination lawsuit, and it was because I had already begun building relationships and transparency that we avoided it. Here is what happened.

We had a period where there was not enough work to ensure that a full line could run every day of the week, let alone multiple lines. There were days where we would furlough people because the work just wasn't there. These are hourly personnel, so their livelihoods are immediately impacted. One of the production managers would give the work to her favorite people. Guess where the people who weren't her favorites were? Lined up at my door because they knew me. I had made myself visible and approachable. They felt discriminated against, and I needed time to figure out what was going on, so I took down their cell numbers and went to investigate. I confirmed that the allegation was true and explained to the supervisor that it can't work that way. People have seniority and differing skill levels, and who she chooses to call can't be a personal decision. People were feeling discriminated against, and it was putting the company at risk for a lawsuit.

I decided to bring the full team in and talk openly about how the rotations would work. We showed them that the new rotation policy was fair and based on seniority and skill. There were machines that certain people were better at running, and so we had to explain to the team that it couldn't be based solely on seniority, because we were

> **Rapport, dialogue, and trust uncover things that you might not have known otherwise, providing you the opportunity to solve them before they become catastrophes.**

trying to rise out of a serious situation by making a better profit by running a line the most productive way possible. We had to be transparent about the problem we were solving for and how we were going to fix it. Some employees still grumbled, but because we were so transparent, and gave the context in which decisions were being made, their negativity couldn't gain any traction.

I also paid attention to that production manager's negative impact moving forward. We counseled her on creating an environment where all people felt valued. Unfortunately, she continued to perpetuate a culture of favoritism, and we had to let her go. I am a strong proponent of doing everything you can before you take that step, but sometimes it is just not possible.

Rapport, dialogue, and trust uncover things that you might not have known otherwise, providing you the opportunity to solve them before they become catastrophes.

Human Resources versus People and Culture

At CGUSA, it's not called Human Resources. It's called People and Culture (P&C). Human resources is the administrative function within people and culture. Human resources is managing the benefits, doing the calculations for workers' comp insurance, meeting with the bank to get the right administrator for the company's 401(k), or running payroll. The components of human resources are clear tasks that need to be done to function. People and culture are about the emotional quotient of the company and its employees. Human resource tasks require an administrator, while P&C requires a leader who engenders trust and knows how to communicate and how to gently counsel people in their harmonizing interactions. That leader is the person who is going to help the individuals in your company navigate the bumps in the road and help them through all the issues that arise. P&C's focus is employee development, morale, and engagement.

That engagement is what I began developing in the early days at CGUSA. I made sure everyone knew who I was and how to find me. Once I demonstrated that I was not only willing but eager to help them, I began to gain their trust. This was the opposite of what Al was doing. It wasn't that Al didn't care about his employees. He was very caring and really had everyone's best interest in mind because he knew they depended on him for their livelihoods. He just didn't have the vision and creativity needed to make it a wonderful place to work. When there is no money for marketing or morale, you must be willing to be creative. Sure, you can give everyone a hundred-dollar bonus at the end of the year and hope that makes them want to stick around for the next twelve months, but rarely is that in and of itself enough.

One of the first wins I was able to garner for the employees was the Good Friday holiday. I had collected some data and saw that over the previous couple of years, the majority of our production workers were calling out sick on Good Friday. Al's solution was to write everyone up for calling in sick. I told him that that wouldn't change anything because Good Friday was a sacred holiday to all of them and so they were still going to call out. Part of creating a positive work environment is acknowledging your employees' personal cultural values. If you don't, they'll leave your company. And then the next group of people will come in, and you'll ignore their values, and they, too, will leave your company. That cycle is costly to your bottom line. I convinced him this was a way for him to be a hero by making it an official company holiday. The employees were thrilled that they didn't have to use paid sick time (there was no paid vacation at this point), and we were able to plan for the downtime more efficiently.

My next win was an easy one. Many employees came to work dressed in costume for Halloween, even though there was nothing special sponsored by the company for the day, so I suggested a Halloween parade and prizes. Prizes cost money, and we had no money. But we did have vendors and, from my Neiman Marcus days, I knew how to use them to my advantage. Most vendors will have money in their budgets for simple giveaways. The other thing I had in my back pocket was American Express points. When I was first helping CGUSA grow out of their problem, I was paying some of their invoices with my business Amex to give CGUSA, in effect, ninety-day terms with vendors, which also gave me Amex points. I cashed in the points for gift cards, and that's what we used for prizes. The employees were so surprised and grateful for the Halloween celebration. Employee engagement in this company-sponsored event became so high we had to make room in the parking lot by moving cars to fit everyone.

I cannot stress enough the need to be creative and look for the small wins. Don't use lack of funds as an excuse not to take care of employee morale.

Those two simple adjustments on management's end boosted morale. People were beginning to look up and smile at each other. It was so heartwarming. We built on that little by little. We would have surprise pizza Fridays or Popsicle Mondays. The biggest evidence of employee engagement and trust in company leadership was when we reinstated paid vacation days. Many long-term employees petitioned me to reinstate paid vacation. I met with them to let them know that at that time it was not possible, but that with their help we could make it happen together. I asked them to take the lead in ensuring high productivity in their respective departments, encourage others to do the same, and eliminate waste, be it idle hours or consumable resources. Simple, but boy, each step really went a long way. They were given the opportunity to be engaged in the solution. Several months later paid vacation time was reinstated. The first time I was invited to a group potluck of the employees, I felt so honored to be included, and it was then that I knew I had done my job.

As rapport and relationships were built, transparency and open discussions became more commonplace. I began seeing more promotions and employee movement between departments. Why? Because they were being noticed, and because they were part of the solutions. Why? Because people were able to talk about their skills and experiences that weren't being utilized. People were growing more confident in sharing their ideas. Internal promotions provided everyone with a visual for their own potential, and so people worked harder so that they, too, could be plucked off the floor and given an opportunity in R&D or quality control or whatever department provided advancement for them. I credit my time at Neiman Marcus for teaching me the value of people and that just because somebody doesn't work out in the job they were hired for, it doesn't mean you should fire them. What it means is you should work with them to understand what's happening. Maybe they're not right for that slot, but they're smart, they're communicative, and they have a strong work ethic, so let's see where they might be a better fit.

Fostering Harmony, Communication, and Trust

When I searched for the head of what became our people and culture department, I drew from the Donna Karan playbook and envisioned a Judy Glaser persona who understood group dynamics and how to personally coach people. Someone who could check in with an employee and say, "Listen, I just wanted to check in with you and give you some feedback about what I saw in the meeting this morning. What I saw in the meeting was that you were uncomfortable, but you weren't talking. Can you tell me why?" and have the employee feel comfortable enough to respond honestly, and the P&C head would be able to provide them support: "Here's a suggestion on how you can bring that up. I'll be in the meeting next week, so I'll be there to support you, and we can get over that hurdle together."

I found the right person. When he first came on board and began coming to meetings in R&D, operations, and sales, people thought, "What is he doing here?" It was a transition, a mind shift, from the human resources concept of hiring and firing and nobody wanting to be called in to human resources to its becoming an integral part of the company's and employees' support system. Enrique enlightened me about why, upon joining the company, he would change the department name from human resources to people and culture. The P&C person must learn about the people and how they work in order to see how they can engage to help further the company goals and culture, and if they're not in those meetings and they're not visible, how will they know? The P&C person can't foster harmony, communication, and trust by sitting in their office doing administrative work. Just as the CEO needs to be visible and approachable to everyone, so, too, does the head of P&C.

Employees need an advocate. Why do you think employees unionize? They don't need a union; they need to be heard and need to know that what they say and feel is considered when policies are made, schedules are changed, etc. They also need direction, structure, support, and to know that they are empowered to be part of the solution. Your P&C head sets the tone for this. They are the chief storyteller of the culture: "We believe that business can be done in a kind, thoughtful, gracious, and generous manner." But the P&C head cannot do it alone. This, your culture, must be embraced and embedded throughout your management team, and they must work in unison proactively through a variety of engagements: intradepartmental group discussions to address challenges, company-wide town hall meetings that provide a forum for employees to ask questions *and* receive answers, and engagement surveys. How are your employees really feeling? Would they recommend to a friend to work there? Each company will find their own path to communication and transparency, but whatever that is for you, be consistent. Walk the talk.

How does one walk the talk? It takes time and experience to develop one's personal values. It takes the influence of others to guide you toward a path that results in your business philosophy. Just like I was molded by my experiences in school, at Neiman Marcus, Donna Karan, L'Oréal and Estee Lauder, each leader will absorb or reject those things that build who they will become. One question to ask yourself as you take the path of leadership is "Am I looking out for the best interest of the company, its employees and client relations, or am

I looking out for my own best interest?" If you answer the latter, find a mentor to help change your perspective; if the former you are well on your way to developing values that will bring success.

What are personal values? They are the underlying motivations you exemplify in the decisions you make and the actions you take. An example can be candor with respect (kindness). How you speak to others shows those you lead that you have their best interest in mind, not your own ego. Another can be transparency with context (honesty and integrity). If you think there is something your employees should know, it's likely that they know already, but without the context you could provide to help either calm their fears or stop the gossip. Another is do what is right even if it shines a light on a mistake you made. This shows you are honorable and have the company's best interest in mind, not your own (humility). There may be times on your path to leadership that these values are not rewarded by those that lead you. These are the hard knocks that hone a person into a good leader. Sometimes it is seeing what not to do that crystalizes the leader you will become.

Your people and culture leader is your best ally for ingraining your values into your company. Transferring these values to others is how you build the culture of your company. Examine your personal business philosophy, establish your company values, and shine a light on them every time you or any one of your employees exemplifies one. This way you build on what you are as a leader and bring others to the next level.

» **Make sure you are visible and accessible to your employees.** They should feel comfortable knocking on your door no matter their level in the company. You should feel comfortable talking to them. If not, start by greeting *everyone*, *every* morning. They need to see you.

» **Let them know what you are doing for them.** More orders means more work for them; more revenue means more stability and better benefits at lower cost for them.

» **Identify your unique culture, establish your values.** Shine a light on exemplification of your values.

» **Overcommunicate.** If there are issues, tell *everyone* on the team about them. You may have some "jumpers," but they wouldn't dig in and help anyway.

» **Know who your mercenaries are.** They are the perpetuators of negativity who look for the rationale for leaving so they don't look bad when they give notice.

» **Care for your team.** Don't let fear of legal booby traps, made ominous in the '80s and '90s, prevent you from being personally engaged with their lives. The reward is rich relationships, a loyal team, and a culture of caring for all involved in your company—employees, clients, and vendors.

» **Culture allows for harmony and balance of all functional areas.**

CHAPTER 8

FUNCTIONAL AREA 7: RISK MANAGEMENT

"What the hell is this?"

I hold the phone away from my ear. "What is what? What's the matter?"

"Al's suing us, that's what's the matter!"

"What the hell are you talking about?" My stomach drops, my mouth suddenly dry.

"Al is claiming that our materials have caused him physical and emotional harm. He's suing us for $1 million. Are you telling me you knew nothing about this?"

"I swear, I know nothing. Send me a copy of the suit. I'm going to try to reach Al." I throw the phone on my desk as if it's poison. I close my eyes and whisper, "What have you done, Al?"

I eye my phone. I hit refresh on my email—Where's that damn suit? There it is. Somehow, I was hoping it would turn out to be some terrible misunderstanding, but no. There it is in black and white: Al is suing our biggest supplier. Now I'm seeing red. I snatch up my phone and call Al. No answer. I leave a voice mail. It's Friday afternoon, and Al has left early to beat the traffic on his long ride home. I call all weekend—he never picks up. He also doesn't come in on Monday, which is when I realize that Al is suing every single one of CGUSA's raw material vendors. Every single one.

Monday morning my phone is ringing off the hook. Every single vendor is calling and telling me that until this gets resolved, they can no longer ship to my company. These are people I have relationships with, I see at trade shows, I've gone to dinner with, who have helped CGUSA recover, and now they're afraid to do business with us. In that moment I am thanking God that I have great legal representation and great liability insurance. I'm so thankful that I intentionally read every contract out loud and in its entirety so that in times like these, I know what it is that I can do.

They Really Are the Good Guys

At this point I was in my second year as CEO, and Al was months away from retiring. One of the last projects he had been working on was the baked-powder pencil, and at one point he asked me if I could provide him the safety data sheets for our raw materials in disc format. When you work in any type of factory that deals with chemicals, by law you must maintain safety data sheets. These tell you not to eat it or get it in your eye, and if there's a fire, this is how you put it out. They also tell you the composition of each material, including how many parts per million or billion you can safely breathe, absorb through the skin, or consume. The company must provide this information to anyone who asks for it. A stranger can walk off the street, enter your building, and request to see the material safety data sheets for your facility. By law you must provide them. One day Al asked me for them, and I directed him to the stack of binders in the warehouse that stores all of them. When he saw how cumbersome they were, he asked if I could put them on a disc for him. I told him sure, because why wouldn't I?

Two months later I had our attorney on one line and our insurance broker on the other, and I was telling them, "Listen, Al's suing our vendors, and they won't ship to us. I need to keep this company running. What are my options?" They bounced it back and forth a bit, trying to figure out if it fell under general liability or if we could put it into the workers' compensation bucket or if we had to get involved at all, since we were not suing or being sued. Really, what they were doing in this moment was talking me off the ledge and providing me options. The attorney was able to quickly confirm that our vendors couldn't refuse to honor their purchase orders with CGUSA as a result of a third-party suit. Al was suing as an individual, CGUSA was not suing anyone, and purchase orders are binding contracts. The attorney helped me think through how to have conversations with our suppliers. In this quick conversation, they did talk me off the ledge and helped me realize that it wasn't as bad as I thought and that we would be able to manage through it.

Now I knew the parameters, and I was able to begin the discussions with my vendors, explaining that we had nothing to do with Al's suit, that he was retiring in a few months, and that we had to remain neutral. The subpoenas, which can be incredibly time consuming, started coming. Their requests sometimes required thousands of emails for which we had to invest time and money to comb through and clear out what was not relevant. Again, this is where you'd better have a strong attorney because a good one will fight back on the subpoenas, and that is exactly what ours did. Our attorney narrowed the scope of their requests by establishing reasonable parameters with each vendor's law firm.

It took time to mend fences with our suppliers, and there were ones we were no longer able to work with going forward. The initial conversations regarding our legally binding purchase orders were a bit of a battle. Not all the vendors took it well when I informed them that they were indeed going to continue shipping to us. Some companies wanted me to sign releases of liability for all the materials they shipped to us. Of course, I wouldn't sign them, because if something was wrong with their materials, then I would have just released liability. In the end we did reformulate some formulas to eliminate those vendors.

It is in these moments that the understanding and relationship you have with your legal representation and your insurance broker are critical. And you can't wait for this type of moment to build this important support team; you must make sure it's in place when everything is humming along smoothly. Attorneys and insurance brokers are not often thought of as the good guys or even as trustworthy at times. But the truth is they are the good guys, and you need them in your corner. Yes, you pay a high commission to your insurance broker and a high hourly rate to your attorney, but when the rubber meets the road, you are so grateful that they are on your team to help you through some of the most trying times in your organization. Treat them as partners, get to know them, and establish a clear understanding of how the relationship is going to work. If your attorney is billing you for every ten minutes or billing you half an hour to read and respond to a thirty-second email, it's up to you to tell them that this can't be how your relationship works. Like any type of relationship,

> **Like any type of relationship, if you put the effort into it, it will work for you.**

if you put the effort into it, it will work for you. And if it's not working, find a new one that will.

Understanding Your Risk Tolerance

Finance and legal go hand in hand. In a small to midsize company, finance handles insurance, rental, employee, and client contracts. Most finance team members can see that a business element of the contract either works or does not, but the "legalese" must be left to the professionals. They see risk *everywhere* and can advise on the scenarios that may bring your company hardship.

Remember when I said that if marketing is running the company, you're lopsided toward marketing and if sales is running the company, you're lopsided toward sales? Sometimes it's a CFO that starts a company, and it becomes all about the bottom line and none of the soft skills or even the marketing skills to build the success on. Now, if legal is running the company, you're hamstrung and your options are limited. Why? Because legal sees risk everywhere. Legal's job is to assess and advise on risk but not to keep you from taking any.

Here is where the CEO and company need to understand their own risk tolerance and determine which what-if scenarios their company can survive. Oftentimes, for midsize organizations, they are desperately trying to budget properly, and so it's about, Do I have enough money for an attorney? Do I have enough money for insurance? What kind of insurance must I have versus what would I like to have to manage risk? Every company would like to have the maximum insurance coverage and an attorney available to review all legal documents, but they're afraid of the cost. Don't assume it's not possible; just have that conversation with the attorney. It's like going to a doctor who's going to charge you $250 a visit. Maybe that's not something you can afford, so you ask what your other options are. It may be that they have a nurse practitioner who is available to treat you at $125 per visit. You find the right thing for your budget and your risk tolerance.

What to Protect

If you're a $1 million company, you're not going to buy $10 million worth of general liability insurance, right? So first you need to determine what your general liability should be: What's the full replacement cost of your essential equipment? That sort of thing. The next critical area of coverage is protecting your company from employees. It is called employment practices insurance, and it covers your company in suits like harassment or wrongful termination claims. It also protects your company if an employee commits fraud in your company that affects a third party. Figuring out what you need is a conversation—really a role-play—with your insurance broker where you talk through what if this happened, or this, or this.

Expect the unexpected. When we had to lay off forty-five people, we did what we could in terms of severance pay. Unfortunately, we had a large group that decided to file a workers' comp claim hoping for thousands of dollars in settlement. They knew they couldn't file a wrongful employment termination suit because I run a highly transparent organization, and everyone knew that we were heading into a tough year and that there would be cuts. So they filed workers' comp lawsuits for cumulative damage to every part of their bodies. Several of them dropped the claim when our investigators explained what fraud would mean for them. If they filed a fraudulent workers' comp lawsuit, they would be subject to criminal and civil charges, would find it extremely difficult to be employed ever again, and could face fines, among other things that are in there to protect employers. In California, however, if you can prove just 1 percent of what you're claiming, you win your lawsuit. You find a doctor that will confirm your claims, and you go into settlement. It took us four years to recover from the effects of those claims, but our insurance broker helped us find a path that wound up actually *saving* CGUSA over a million dollars over those four years. Thanks, Chuck!

If your broker is not willing to go through all those scenarios with you or they get exasperated doing so, you have the wrong insurance agent. Your broker should be willing to walk you through every single possible scenario that could happen and then help you determine your risk factor. You may have a high tolerance for risk and think the risk of your employees filing a claim is low, so you decide you don't need much employment practices insurance. Or you just spent millions on tenant improvements to your facility. Your building is in an earthquake zone, but the risks of earthquake are low, but do you want to risk your investment?

Tap into your advisors when assessing for insurance needs. For many CEOs that will be their board. What do they see as potential risk scenarios, and what's their comfort level for coverage? If the buck stops with you and there is no board, you need to reach out to colleagues and friends who are in the industry to gain insight and figure out the right questions to ask your broker. The other part of the equation is, Does your insurance broker understand your business? If not, it would be difficult for them to provide you industry-specific insights—another reason to gather advisor insights. There are brokers who specialize in specific industries. My broker specializes in manufacturing. That doesn't mean he specializes in cosmetics, but he's well versed in manufacturing and will understand what CGUSA needs. Insurance agents are paid on commission. They want to sell you as much insurance as they can, but the good ones will only sell you what you need. Do your research and due diligence, and find the broker that works best for you.

Contracts, Contracts, Contracts

Are you in the habit of signing blank checks? I thought not. That's what contracts are when you read them in a hurry, in between meetings and emails, and without consultation: a blank check. Contracts are binding, so you need to understand what you're signing and be able to repeat it back to somebody as if it's a test. Most CEOs should know about every single contract. They should have read every single one, and they should understand every single one. People are often intimidated by the legalese, but the truth is the majority of your contracts are not legal decisions. They are business decisions that are legally binding. It becomes a legal issue only when you choose not to uphold a business decision that you contractually agreed to.

No matter how amazing your attorney is, they are going to focus on the legal aspects of the contracts, like representations and warranties and whether you have the right to enter into this contract. But if the contract says your vendor is going to sell you this product at this price for the next five years, that's business. Review of your contracts by a legal professional is critical, but it is not enough.

Contracts in companies request different things. It may be a business decision that has to do with routing—What are the shipping requirements? There are financial considerations—Are you going to give a rebate of 2 percent if they pay you in ten days? What are the quality standards that the contract requires? Yes, I am going to say it again: *running a company is a team sport.* You must have your quality control person review the contract to see if there is anything that you can't accommodate or shouldn't accommodate, or if you accommodate it, should you be asking for compensation? Pull finance in to determine what the bottom-line cost will be if you agree to a 2 percent rebate. Before you agree to shipping parameters, you'd better make sure operations agrees that you can accommodate them. Know your contracts. When I say read it out loud, I really mean read it out loud, because you can't skim something when you read it out loud. You have to say all the words. Every word matters. Sometimes one little word can wreak legal havoc and result in lost revenue.

The moral here is that you need to know your risks and risk tolerance and put the right insurance broker and attorney in place to help you manage those risks. You will know you have the right ones in place when they treat you like a partner, not a paycheck.

Quality Control and Assurance

Yes, you have a quality department. Yes, they have standard operating procedures for just about everything. Yes, they are generally seen as the "cops" of your business. Quality control and assurance is everyone's job. As such, they are a part of every functional area. They provide the structure for how you perform against the expectations of your clients, regulatory bodies, and your own standards, for everything. The quality of materials brought into the company, the standards your vendors must live up to, the quality and repeatability of the products you make, the quality of how they are made. Your quality department impacts how items are priced in order to maintain company quality standards and client expectations, which impacts sales, marketing, R&D, finance, and operations. Quality is part of legal agreements. Quality is like an invisible net around your company. Why invisible? Because it is so ingrained into every functional area that it blends in.

Your quality department protects your company, your clients, and the end user. They train and retrain everyone in myriad of standard operating procedures to ensure all in the company are empowered to maintain quality standards. They are the record keepers of the care you take at every stage of production and the tests that show that product safety parameters have been met and can provide the shield that prevents environment requirements from putting your company at risk.

At CGUSA we manufacture in California, which has strict environmental requirements. One of these is wastewater production, which includes runoff from our building during a rainstorm (yes, it does rain in Southern California, and when it does, it pours). We are required to sample runoff rainwater on the first rain day of any period. After one particular rain, we received a warning that we had high zinc (a heavy metal) in our runoff water. The regulatory body thought we were emitting this zinc through our production process. We were at risk of being shut down if we did not reduce the zinc in our runoff rainwater. We knew we were not emitting zinc in our process but needed to find out what was causing it. Quality enlisted the help of our engineers and our chemists in R&D to think through the issue and discover what could possibly be happening to cause it. After a second rain and a second warning, we were at a loss. Until we went up on the roof of the building and realized that the new solar panels were attached with zinc fittings to lessen the weight on the roof. Quality worked with engineering to coat the fittings to solve for the zinc runoff and prevent a company shutdown. Phew!

» Make sure you have a legal advisor and an insurance agent who *understand* your business, your risk tolerance, and your needs.

» Take notes and ask questions of your agent, attorney, and finance team even if you have already blindly signed contracts.

» Read every last word of every contract *out loud* to someone else. Active listening is critical here.

» If the contract speaks to various departments, make sure that department weighs in on the verbiage and agreement elements.

» If you haven't already, read all your insurance and legal contracts now!

» Recognize the great service your quality department is doing for you. Often they are the unsung heroes that save the day.

CHAPTER 9

FUNCTIONAL AREA 8: BOARD OF DIRECTORS

O ne board member said, "Everyone needs to take a 20 percent salary cut!" Then another said, "It's time to lay off the staff." Still another: "What about the offices? Surely you can get out of the lease!" Then, practically in unison: "You hired a consultant?!"

It was my first board meeting with one of my first clients after opening my consultancy. I thought, Wow, the room is already on fire. I had made it through ten minutes of my presentation, and their hands were already firmly wrapped around the hatchet, ready to cut, cut, cut. I was there to present spend, spend, spend.

This company had turned to friends, family, local businesses, banks, and one investment professional to raise money. In exchange for angel investment, all of them were given shares of the company and seats on the board. Two years in, the company had a few boutique distributors, six stores of a national retailer who carried their brand for sale, and little hope of saving the investors' money. I was hired to greatly expand this brand's product distribution to generate cash, which required spending on marketing, sales teams, and product production. Clearly, this hostile board was not prepared to hear the plan.

Boards are often filled with smart, powerful people who are used to being in control. As board members, they have no control over how the CEO runs the company. They generally can fire you whenever they want to, but on a day-to-day basis, they don't control what you do. They're not pushing all the buttons and moving all the needles and doing everything you're doing. That can lead to fear, which can lead to hostility. It's up to you to help identify the fear behind their hostility, and then you can approach them with understanding and with your most logical and analytical explanation of why they don't need to be afraid. Fear of risk, fear of failure, fear of the unknown: Whatever the fear is, when not addressed, it leads to a lot of the disruption and chaos in a business. Developing a relationship with each board member will provide valuable insight into their mindset so that you can address issues before they become hostile.

A little civility goes a long way to defuse hostilities.

How could I rewind this hostile board meeting? I didn't know that each of these board members was also an investor. I didn't know which were family and which were not. I didn't know that most were unaware that I had been hired. Okay, let's start there.

"I'm sorry, let me back up," I said. "Perhaps we can start over with introductions, a recap of my last three weeks, and why I was hired." A little civility goes a long way to defuse hostilities. Knowing who they were, what they worried about, and how I could eventually help brought the hostilities to an end.

Sounding Board

It's lonely at the top! But it doesn't have to be. Your board can be a great sounding board, no pun intended. They can help you think through a problem, give advice outside of your board meetings, and be a source of connection to people that can help your company in a myriad of ways. The more you engage with them, the better you will all align on corporate guidance, the stronger your relationship with them will be, and the more productive and impactful your board meetings will be.

At CGUSA our board of directors consists of three members. CGUSA is a family-owned business, and so in this circumstance, the board includes two nonemployee family members and me, the company CEO. I apprise them of what is happening within the company, but we also value each other as sounding boards to determine strategies moving forward. Should we invest in more automation? How do we compensate for out-of-state competitors paying $7.29 per hour while we are paying $15 an hour minimum wage? Insurance is always a big one. Whether it's general liability, workers' comp, fire, flood, earthquake, or medical insurance, the exorbitant costs require multiple risk scenarios. Where we are located in California, we are at risk of fire or earthquakes. In my case the board members are owners, and when we strategize, we are talking about the value of their organization and the value of their investment, and as the CEO, I need to understand how they feel about protecting it and their tolerance to risk.

Board members can help you gain perspective on an issue, like a matter involving an employee, a competitor, or a prospective client, or even another board member. If a board member in your company is not coping well with a challenge the company is facing, sometimes a private conversation outside the boardroom is enough to defuse one member's bad day, but what if it's not? Check in with other members. Are they seeing things the same way you are? Maybe other members are feeling the same but they are just not as vocal. Perhaps this member is no longer a fit for the board, or perhaps they are operating based on a fear that you need to identify and help allay. Most important is alignment; without it, discord and chaos are lurking around the corner.

Building a Board

It's true that you may have been hired onto an existing board whose members won't be changing anytime soon, but if you do have the opportunity to select new members or build a board from scratch, here are some to-dos.

» Ensure that the number of total members is odd to avoid stalemates.

» Fill seats to make up for your areas of weakness. If you're not great at finance, find a member who is. If you're new to the industry, find a member that has been successful in it.

» Background checks and references are expected. Don't be apologetic or embarrassed. Anyone that pushes back on that should not become part of your board. In fact, professionals who are top captains of their industry are going to be impressed that you are being this careful. Transparency is critical.

» To the extent possible, the full board should interview every potential board member to see how they gel with the group. You want a board that can have discussions and disagreements but still be productive for the good of the company.

» Choose committed and experienced members.

» Get to know your members outside of the board room. What is their philosophy of business? If yours is like mine, "Business can be done in a kind, thoughtful, gracious, and generous manner," and theirs is, "It's business; empathy doesn't belong here," you may not want them on your board, *or* you may strategically place them on the board to keep a balance. Discover their area of expertise, how they conduct their own business, and their reputation as a board member for other entities.

When I faced a board that was ready to cut, cut, cut, my job was to gain alignment to spend, spend, spend instead. Luckily, the opposition was mostly based on fear. They didn't really want to gut the company of talent and opportunity. They were willing to take calculated risks to recoup their investments and help their families' and friends' company succeed. This company had board members that aligned with their philosophy but not yet their strategy. Choose your board members with care, and if you're not choosing them, make sure *your* philosophy meshes with theirs before you agree to come on board.

Know When It's Time to Leave a Party

Let's say you are not doing the choosing but are being interviewed by an existing board. Ask the right questions and, hopefully, you will receive honest answers so you know what you are walking into. If you don't have the opportunity to meet most of the board members, get your research on. Who are they (background, experience)? What drives them (family, personal friend, investor)? Why are they on this board (retired, being paid for special expertise, personal interest engagement)? On what other boards do they serve? They need to know you too. Be transparent about your philosophy in the interview. If you are mostly aligned, then join the party and keep on pushing for your beliefs/plans/ideas. If you are not aligned and perhaps the paycheck is huge but you don't feel like it's a good match—dang, that's painful; don't accept the invitation. If you thought you were a match when you accepted but months later realize you aren't? You are now either a warrior for change or you need to thank them for inviting you to the party and bow out gracefully. It's important to know when it's time to leave. Own your mistake in person to the board. You never know, they may want your brand of philosophy but don't know how to get there. If this is the case, recommend a third-party consultant to help effect change on the board.

Advice Worth Taking

Sometimes companies are not ready for a formal board, or sometimes you may have voting board members *and* advisory board members. An advisory board operates very similarly to a formal board except that advisors are not officers or directors of the company.

> » **Build and utilize your advisory board.** The CGUSA board chose an advisory board of four members. Since CGUSA was short on marketing, we selected the former CMO of Coty. For a global perspective, we chose the former general manager for the Americas from Johnson & Johnson. For finance we chose the former CFO of Elizabeth Arden. And for corporate guidance, we chose the former CEO of Revlon. All strong leaders from within the cosmetics industry who could help us grow.

> » **Pay your board of directors and your advisory board members.** You must pay people who are willing to invest their time and

expertise in your company. Determine how much time you need from them and how much you can afford to pay. At CGUSA we ask our advisory board members to meet once per year, and they also make themselves available for advice and consultation as needed throughout the year. We pay our advisory board members, and it has been my experience that most members want their pay donated to a charity. Even when that is the case, the acknowledgment of paying for their valuable time and insights is important.

When I became CEO of CGUSA, I was fortunate to be able to choose one of the three advisory board members. I chose Paul West, the former CFO of Elizabeth Arden and former COO of Unilever. I had been introduced to Paul early in my career and, as my own business grew, I stayed in touch over the years. Paul has a successful history with various organizations in the industry, he has provided me great advice, and we have a personal relationship, so for me he was the perfect choice. The chairman of our board found the other three advisory board members through various philanthropic events and projects in which he has been involved. Like me, he had developed a personal relationship with these individuals and came to know that their experience at Revlon, Johnson & Johnson, and Coty and their skill set, philosophy, and intentions were in line with CGUSA.

Now, not everyone will have access to that level of individual for their advisory board, nor do they need to. A company may reach out to somebody who runs a smaller company than those, who has consulted for years in the industry, or who they may have met at an

It may still feel lonely sometimes, but you're not alone when you have a board of directors or an advisory board.

event or worked with at one time. As you grow in your career, you call that person and tell them that you are establishing an advisory board and you think they will be a great asset to the company, and share some information on what you are doing and how you can compensate them.

It may still feel lonely sometimes, but you're not alone when you have a board of directors or an advisory board.

» **If you don't have a choice of who your board members are, research, research, research.** You need to *know* who they are and how well your business philosophy aligns with theirs.

» **If you are able to choose your board members, don't get star-struck.** Background checks and references are critical.

» ***You* may not be the right fit.** If that's the case, own it and bow out gracefully.

» **Advisory boards are a great way to get informal help for your company.**

CHAPTER 10

BREAKOUT

You don't know what you don't know. I know that sounds cliché, but the truth is it's the most valuable lesson I learned way back in my Neiman Marcus days. Had I been closed off to information, new ideas, or change, I might never have gotten out of the gift wrap department of Neiman Marcus or become a CEO, for that matter. When you're willing to recognize that there are things you simply don't know, you open yourself to a whole world of information and differing perspectives and you empower yourself with knowledge that allows you to create, to solve, to innovate. In my role as merchandise coordinator for cosmetics at Neiman Marcus, I was like a student of social anthropology studying the beliefs, cultural engagement, and economic arrangement of the cosmetics industry.

That exposure and my fascination with it are what led me on the path to lifelong learning and evolution. In that first management position, I was a young woman in her twenties enrolled in an English literature master's degree program and a business minor while tasked with figuring out how to convince a group of salespeople in their forties and fifties that what they saw as a dearth of product available for them to sell was in fact a golden opportunity. Yes, I was nervous, but I was also willing to learn and eager to put into practice all the information I'd gathered from my college business courses, my Neiman Marcus executive courses, and my own observations.

So now it's time to take a leap into accepting that things may need to change in your organization while also recognizing and celebrating the things that are going great. There must be joy and celebration, not fear, in the steps that you choose to take. This breakout chapter provides you concrete steps you can take right now. Let's get to work!

Breakout One: Marketing

1. **Where to start?** Whether you are launching a new company or growing an existing one, you must start at the beginning. Who *are* you as a company? What do you *want to be* as a company? If these two answers are aligned, great. You are ready to move on to step two. If not, fill the gap. What needs to be done to get from where you are to where you want to be? Make a list of what is preventing you from getting there, and work that list every day.

2. **Know who and where your customers are and how to reach them.** Your employees are your best amplification resource. Ignite their pride and passion for your product, service, and company and encourage them to shout it from the rooftops ... where your customers are, whether on LinkedIn, Instagram, TikTok, Facebook, or some other platform, like trade shows.

3. **Data, data, data.** Mine it, analyze it, and use it to continuously hone your message. Things change, people change, and

trends change. Stay on top of the change via online industry articles, publicly traded competitors' corporate filings, and your clients' publicly traded filings. For CGUSA, if we see our that our customer's client announced in their corporate filing that they intend to grow their revenue via online sales and a 25 percent increase of in-house generic brands, that gives my team time to strategize with our customer to fill the online portion and perhaps provide a new channel as a supplier for their client's in-house brand.

4. **Set a lower budget than you want to.** Why? Testing the results. Launch your marketing test and collect and analyze the information. If the strategy worked, wash, rinse, and repeat. If your goal was a 1 percent return on a promotional ad and you hit a 2 percent return—hooray! Now analyze the data and figure out what moved the needle. Was it a word, a discount, a trend you hit? Or maybe it was run on a payday Friday. Test it again, and compare the results.

5. **Remember, marketing is a team sport.** Always include the ideas, experiences, and comments from your other departments.

Breakout Two: Sales

1. **Customer experience is everything!** Do a personal test run as a customer. Was it easy to find parking? Was the customer welcomed quickly and warmly when they entered? How long before they received assistance? Ask someone who knows nothing about your business to navigate your website. Was it easy, confusing, frustrating? Did they have fun? You get the picture.

2. **Sales is not just about dollars and cents.** It's about creating relationships and growing them. Take a look at your sales culture. Is it all about the big win, or are your sales team members rewarded on long-term repeat customers and productive sales?

3. **Customer feedback is key.** Find a way to obtain it. Pick up the phone and ask. Send out a three-question survey. Ask for an in-person meeting that is all about them and what you can do to help.

4. **Then be there ready to help.** You want to be your client's first phone call.

Breakout Three: Research and Product Development

1. **Always ask *why*.** Why should we make this product? Why is it better? Why is it desirable? Why will it win? Why will it help the company's bottom line? Why hasn't anyone ever ... ?

2. **Develop your *how*.** Once you have your why, it's time to develop your plan of *how* to make your product safe, affordable, functional, scalable, and profitable.

3. **Stay alert.** The second you launch your product, others are already improving upon it. Go from new to *new and improved*!

4. **Do not operate in a vacuum.** Product development is a collaborative process. Marketing, sales, finance, operations, quality, and legal must be included in the why and the how.

5. **Product development must be conscious of market price.** What will the market bear? It must be priced right so there is room for return on investment.

Breakout Four: Finance & Data Analysis

1. **Get to know your finance team.** Make sure they know that their mission is to help you find the cracks that leak profits and identify areas of excellence that are hyperprofitable. Finance turns everything that is done in the company into numbers that provide a report card of how well the company is doing. Harness that power to help all departments achieve an A+.

2. **Find an Excel wizard.** If your company is not ready for an ERP system, that's okay. Find an Excel expert to create the dashboards you need. Compare and assess your company's past, present, and future trajectory.

3. **Know how to read a balance sheet and how to analyze the data it contains.** Year-over-year comparisons may happily surprise you or shock you. No cash? The balance sheet will help understand you where it went—inventory, loans on assets, shareholder distributions, tenant improvements? Armed with current information, you are ready to plan for next steps.

Breakout Five: People & Culture

1. **Strengthen your people and culture.** If your "human resources" department is providing only administrative functions like payroll, benefits, and workers' comp, it's time to level up. Strengthen P&C with employee engagement, trust, counseling, and development.

2. **Be transparent.** If you have ever asked yourself, "Should I tell my employees (fill in the blank)?" chances are they already know, but what they think they know is wrong, diluted, or blown out of proportion. If you want your team to respect you and stand with you, always communicate with them honestly.

3. **Choose your P&C partner wisely.** They must be your mirror who is willing to reflect back to you the good, the bad, and the ugly and then help you promote it or solve for it. They are your greatest ally.

4. **Do nice things for your employees—without them, your company would not exist.** This will help with employee engagement when *you* need *them*.

Breakout Six: Operations, Inventory, & Supply Chain

1. **Discover your KPIs (key performance indicators).** What is that you do, make, sell, or provide that turns into cash? How does it turn into cash? How does it turn into more cash? What prevents it from turning into the most cash possible? Gather that data and triage it. Are you bleeding out? Stop the bleeding, now! Are you gaining extra weight? Get disciplined and streamline. Healthy? Great! Do *more* of whatever you are doing. Good, bad, or status quo—record your progress. No one wants to hear, "Wait, what did we do to make that work?!"

2. **Listen to your operations team.** If your supply chain can't get it, you can't promote it or sell it. When marketing and sales

try to sell unavailable products, all your company is doing is making empty promises. Product development—listen to your engineers and manufacturing team. Believe me, they want to make it just as much as you do. If they say, "It just can't be done," don't give up. Be curious, ask why, understand the limitations, work together toward a solution, and remember that solutions are around the corner.

3. **Help your ops team succeed!** They are not servants who need to adjust to your—or your client's—every whim. They make you shine and look like you made the impossible happen, so appreciate them. Nine times out of ten, the operations team are the ones who save the day. Give them the credit they deserve and a seat at the company's strategy table.

Breakout Seven: Risk Management

1. **Take out each and every contract that you have signed and read them out loud, and before you sign another one, read *it* out loud.** If the terms no longer work for you, it's time to renegotiate.

2. **Believe that your attorneys and insurance brokers are the good guys on your team.** Develop relationships with them *before* the panic moment of need.

3. **Establish your risk tolerances and how much you are willing to pay to reduce them.**

4. **If contracts speak to various department's deliverables, make sure to review those with the department head.** You may find that the contract reach is too far based on the expertise of the department leaders.

Breakout Eight: Board of Directors

1. **Establish an advisory board even if you don't yet have or need a board of directors.**

2. **Identify your weaknesses and fill those gaps with members of the board of directors and advisory board.**

3. **Determine the most effective and efficient board of directors meeting schedule.** That may be monthly, quarterly, or annually. If three months go by and most things remain the same, then twice a year may be right for you. If a three-month period sees so much activity that you are going off the rails, then monthly is best.

4. **Don't be afraid to push back on the board.** Remember, however, that humility and diplomacy coupled with data gain the most respect. Ego gets you fired or makes board members lose interest.

> Humility and diplomacy coupled with data gain the most respect.

CONCLUSION

I used to sit around the kitchen table with my dad and talk business. There were many times when the exhaustion of not getting a promotion or feeling like I had failed at something or nagging self-doubt or just lacking the vision to see what the next path could be would take over, and I'd say, "You know, Dad, this is it. Where I am today is as far as I'm going to go in my career." He would get so mad and sternly remind me that I could do anything. He'd tell me to reach out to one of my counterparts from one of my old companies and see what they were doing—this was old-school networking, long before LinkedIn and Facebook. Then he'd tell me to find something new to learn and use it to propel myself forward. My dad was an entrepreneur at heart, and he passed that enterprising spirit on to me.

If there is only one message you take away from my story, let it be *keep your entrepreneurial spirit alive*. Never lose your curiosity that drives you to ask, "What's next?" "What can I do better?" "How can I learn from that mistake?" "Who can help me?" "Who can I teach what I know so we can all rise?" Be willing to take risks. You can't be an entrepreneur and always play it safe. Most of all, embrace change.

Just when you think you have figured it all out, all functional areas are in balance, and you hit cruise control on the dial, it all changes. Sometimes you see the change coming; sometimes you don't. A critical leadership team member relocates for family reasons, and you have to onboard a new one who may need time to harmonize with the rest of the team; a top client may hit their own snag that greatly impacts your company; the government might increase minimum wage by 45 percent; a trend may quickly change, either creating a great opportunity or making your product obsolete; a worldwide pandemic may hit, and you have to pivot to survive. The entrepreneur at heart who embraces change will catch these curveballs, since they are generally ready to disrupt the status quo anyway.

Lifelong learning is the best way to keep the entrepreneurial spirit alive. Learning comes in many forms, be it higher education; immersing yourself in books, books, and more books; or the experience of doing. Educational opportunities abound. You just need to be aware and take the opportunity when it's presented.

Starting so young as the gift wrap girl at Neiman Marcus while attending college primed me for finding the lessons wherever I could. College was teaching me critical analysis and creative thinking. So steeped was I in process at school, I couldn't help but apply it to work. What solutions would make a situation better? How could I understand the ins and outs of inventory and solve the puzzle of loss? How can I fix a dying cosmetics department? Learn, apply it, give back, teach.

It's up to you to find the balance by cultivating a supportive environment built on trust and harmony. A team of incredibly intelligent people are only as good as their interactions with each other. You must give yourself and your team permission to speak and share freely, with care, without judgment, because one idea may spark something in someone else, and now you have something to build on together. Interaction, engagement, communication, trust, nonjudgment—all these things matter to bring your company into balance, to have the harmony that creates company success.

Stay aware and open to all that is possible, assess the risks, and then take action—do not wait until the stars align and everything is perfect, because that time will never come. Take action today.

ACKNOWLEDGMENTS

I want to acknowledge and thank the many people who have told me over the years that I should write a book. With each passing year and new experience those voices culminated into a crescendo that I could not ignore. Clients, friends, family, and coworkers have all contributed to the force that brought this book to life.

First, I want to thank my husband Tom whose unconditional love and steadfast support has given me the strength and confidence that helped me through the challenging experiences which are the subject of this book. And thank you to my sons Michael and Eric who show me that the Balancing Act of Business principles apply at home too. Family is a team sport.

My thanks to Sue Mitchell of The Barrett Group for her years as my career coach. She helped me crystalize my thinking about the business challenges I faced so that I could put my experiences into actions that helped my clients, helped me grow as a leader, and helped me write this book.

A special note of thanks to my cousin Betsy who has been my life coach, best friend, and ardent supporter of this book.

Thank you to Beth Cooper of Advantage Media Group who helped me with the voice and outline of this book. Her constant feedback and writings kept me on track and focused. I could not have written this without her.

My gratitude goes out to the many coworkers, clients, leaders, and mentors who have touched my life and career. All have taught me the value of giving back and are the reason this book exists.

CPSIA information can be obtained
at www.ICGtesting.com
Printed in the USA
JSHW081811290623
44008JS00003B/13